SS PASTEUR / TS BREMEN

CLASSIC LINERS

SS PASTEUR / TS BREMEN

ANDREW BRITTON

The
History
Press

I dedicate the book to Jim McFaul, who has inspired and encouraged me to write it. He is a devoted maritime enthusiast who works tirelessly as a volunteer for the World Ship Society.

Cover illustrations: front: The TS *Bremen* is pictured entering Quebec in Canada in August 1971. (Marc Piche); rear: An impressive view across the Hudson River at New York on 11 June 1940 with SS *Pasteur* in the centre. (Richard Weiss Collection)

First published 2015

The History Press
The Mill, Brimscombe Port
Stroud, Gloucestershire, GL5 2QG
www.thehistorypress.co.uk

© Andrew Britton, 2015

The right of Andrew Britton to be identified as the Author of this work has been asserted in accordance with the Copyright, Designs and Patents Act 1988.

British Library Cataloguing in Publication Data.
A catalogue record for this book is available from the British Library.

ISBN 978 0 7509 6101 1

Typesetting and origination by The History Press
Printed in China

Contents

Acknowledgements

Tremendous encouragement and international support have been received in the writing of this book. This includes access to historical information and photographical material from William Tilley and Richard Weiss of the United States who are devoted enthusiasts of the *Pasteur* and TS *Bremen*. Considerable assistance has been obtained from Hal Stolen, who is the host of the Internet website devoted to the *Pasteur*, www.stolenworks.com, and also to former TS *Bremen* crew member Rolf Heimig, who manages the superb website devoted to the ship, www.ts-bremen.de. The Canadian maritime historian, Gordon Turner, very generously mailed to me a large package of original historical documents and artefacts relating to the ship to assist with research and illustrations for the book. I can not thank Gordon enough. Additionally the Associated Press has been extremely helpful in providing me with negatives and original prints of the ship covering the career of the ship.

Special mention must be made of two other maritime stalwarts from the USA: David Boone and Ernest Arroyo have dipped into their archives to assist with photographic illustrations for this book.

Many friends have helped by allowing me to include their original work and several have generously donated this material. I am indebted to Graham Cocks for the generous gift of all his slides to this project. Barry Eagles, Richard Weiss, Marche Piche, Bill Cotter, Clive Harvey and William Tilley have also given permission for their fabulous colour slides to be included and I am very grateful to them. William Tilley has also been a source of great inspiration and encouragement with his enthusiasm and knowledge of the SS *Pasteur*/TS *Bremen*. He has provided me with much historical information about the ship and directed me to many sources of information, for which I owe a great debt of thanks.

I must also extend my sincere thanks to Richard Weiss, William Paulus and Clive Harvey for providing me with a mass of black-and-white negatives and original photographs of the ship to use.

I owe a great debt of thanks to Jim McFaul of the World Ship Society for his considerable assistance in locating colour slides for this book.

I would like to extend my sincere thanks to the National Records Office at Kew and Her Majesty's Ministry of Defence for providing me with considerable freedom to explore stored information and original records relating to the ship during her early service and in the Second World War. After delving through endless boxes of original records, my eyes almost popped out as I discovered the original records for the SS *Pasteur* and SS *Nieuw Amsterdam*, which had been hidden away and forgotten about since 1946. These unique records will become Crown copyright and be relocated to the National Archive at Kew and it is intended they will be open to public inspection at a future date when catalogued.

Stern magazine of Germany have been extremely helpful in providing me with scans of the dramatic sinking of the ship, which were taken by Frans Schepers from aboard the tug *Sumatra*. Sadly, they can not locate the original slides which were published in an article in *Stern* in 1980. Despite strenuous efforts by *Stern* magazine, the World Ship Society, Hal Stolen, Rolf Heimig and me, it has been impossible to trace the original

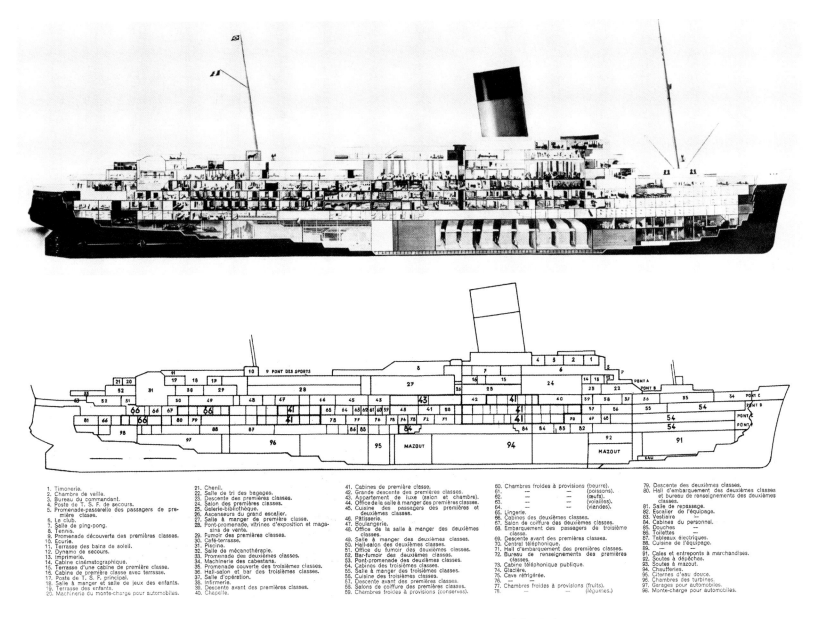

1. Timonerie.
2. Chambre de veille.
3. Bureau du commandant.
4. Poste de T. S. F. de secours.
5. Promenade-passerelle des passagers de première classe.
6. Le club.
7. Salle de ping-pong.
8. Tennis.
9. Promenade découverte des premières classes.
10. Ecurie.
11. Terrasse des bains de soleil.
12. Dynamo de secours.
13. Imprimerie.
14. Cabine cinématographique.
15. Terrasse d'une cabine de première classe.
16. Cabine de première classe avec terrasse.
17. Poste de T. S. F. principal.
18. Salle à manger et salle de jeux des enfants.
19. Terrasse des enfants.
20. Machinerie du monte-charge pour automobiles.

21. Chenil.
22. Salle de tri des bagages.
23. Descente des premières classes.
24. Salon des premières classes.
25. Galerie-bibliothèque.
26. Ascenseurs du grand escalier.
27. Salle à manger de première classe.
28. Pont-promenade, vitrines d'exposition et magasins de vente.
29. Fumoir des premières classes.
30. Café-terrasse.
31. Piscine.
32. Salle de mécanothérapie.
33. Promenade des deuxièmes classes.
34. Machinerie des cabestans.
35. Promenade couverte des troisièmes classes.
36. Hall-salon et bar des troisièmes classes.
37. Salle d'opération.
38. Infirmerie.
39. Descente avant des premières classes.
40. Chapelle.

41. Cabines de première classe.
42. Grande descente des premières classes.
43. Appartement de luxe (salon et chambre).
44. Office de la salle à manger des premières classes.
45. Cuisine des passagers des premières et deuxièmes classes.
46. Pâtisserie.
47. Boulangerie.
48. Office de la salle à manger des deuxièmes classes.
49. Salle à manger des deuxièmes classes.
50. Hall-salon des deuxièmes classes.
51. Office du fumoir des deuxièmes classes.
52. Bar-fumoir des deuxièmes classes.
53. Pont-promenade des deuxièmes classes.
54. Cabines des troisièmes classes.
55. Salle à manger des troisièmes classes.
56. Cuisine des troisièmes classes.
57. Descente avant des premières classes.
58. Salons de coiffure des premières classes.
59. Chambres froides à provisions (conserves).

60. Chambres froides à provisions (beurre).
61. — — — (poissons).
62. — — — (œufs).
63. — — — (volailles).
64. — — — (viandes).
65. Lingerie.
66. Cabines des deuxièmes classes.
67. Salon de coiffure des deuxièmes classes.
68. Embarquement des passagers de troisième classe.
69. Descente avant des premières classes.
70. Central téléphonique.
71. Hall d'embarquement des premières classes.
72. Bureau de renseignements des premières classes.
73. Cabine téléphonique publique.
74. Glacière.
75. Cave réfrigérée.
76. —
77. Chambres froides à provisions (fruits).
78. — — — (légumes.)

79. Descente des deuxièmes classes.
80. Hall d'embarquement des deuxièmes classes et bureau de renseignements des deuxièmes classes.
81. Salle de repassage.
82. Escalier de l'équipage.
83. Vestiaire.
84. Cabines du personnel.
85. Douches —
86. Toilettes —
87. Tableaux électriques.
88. Cuisine de l'équipage.
89. —
91. Cales et entrepôts à marchandises.
92. Soutes à dépêches.
93. Soutes à mazout.
94. Chaufferies.
95. Citernes d'eau douce.
96. Chambres des turbines.
97. Garages pour automobiles.
98. Monte-charge pour automobiles.

SS *Pasteur* cutaway cross-section in 1939. (Britton Collection)

Proud shipbuilders and their families line the shore to cheer and wave following the launch of the SS *Pasteur* on 15 February 1938. (Britton Collection)

The TS *Bremen* is pictured passing the record-breaking SS *United States* off the Battery, on the Hudson River, New York, in November 1969. (Britton Collection)

photographer. If Frans Schepers reads this, please contact me direct via the publisher.

As always, my friend and neighbour Michael Jakeman has thoroughly checked the content of this book. I would like to express my appreciation for all his time, support and generous assistance.

I am extremely grateful to my brother-in-law Mike Pringle who meticulously scanned each and every slide. This amounts to months of unseen hard work. Without his help, this book and the whole series would not have come into being. I also owe my sister Ruth a massive thank you for all her patience and encouragement. A special thank you should go to my wife Annette who spent many hours and days translating from French and German for me. My sons Jonathan, Mark and Matthew are also owed a great debt of thanks for encouraging me and putting up with masses of colour slides, boxes of ocean liner logbooks and shipping artefacts.

Introduction

From my childhood days I have vivid memories of the North German Lloyd TS *Bremen* regularly sailing across the Solent and up Southampton Water. I watched her many times majestically sail past Hythe Pier and dock in the New Docks whilst eating my fish and chips or tucking into a waterside picnic. A family sightseeing visit around Southampton Docks brought me into close contact with this beautiful liner at sea level and I recall watching a team of painters, balanced precariously on a plank, hard at work with their brushes and pots. My next encounter with the TS *Bremen* was a nocturnal one, when visiting my Uncle Joe who was busy working unloading a liner in the docks. She looked very distinctive with her illuminated prominent mustard-coloured funnel and black hull. This impressive ship left a deep impression on me and I determined with my father that the next time we saw the *Bremen* we would find an excuse to venture aboard for a visit.

A full year passed and the family paid a visit to meet up with a neighbour who was working on board the P & O *Oriana*. After a tour of this wonderful cruise liner, we were invited to the ship next door, the TS *Bremen*. I climbed the gangway up onto the great German liner with some excitement. We were warmly greeted at the entrance to the ship by an officer and as we stepped onto the plush thick welcome mat we were welcomed aboard. 'What a wonderful ship and how luxurious' was the thought in my head at the time. She had a unique style and her interior finish was quite superb, with a lot of polished wood and brass. As we slowly wandered around the ship she conveyed an air of refined German discipline and order yet one of an elegant atmosphere.

Slowly making our way along the spectacular promenade decks and down the corridors of the ship, I noticed an amusing sight. Outside many of the closed cabin doors were passenger's shoes. My father whispered in my ear that the shoes had been left outside by passengers so that they could be polished. Next we received a very cordial invitation to visit the bridge from a smiling gentleman in uniform who was being followed by a small dog. On entering the bridge, there was a distinctive smell of polish, and the linoleum floor gleamed like glass. The uniformed gentleman, now stroking the dog in his arms, explained the full workings of the ship to my father and me. I was almost spellbound after about 15 minutes, and the gentleman invited us down to the first-class restaurant. Upon learning from my father that our family were associated with the British Cunard Line, this warm-hearted gentleman then revealed his identity. He was none other than Captain Günter Rössing. 'Please join me for some Christmas refreshments,' the jovial Captain said. Turning to my father, he smiled and added, 'Feel free to have anything you wish; caviar, lobster, German Champagne'. As we sat quietly admiring the magnificent place settings with finest crystal, polished china and crisp white linens with fresh sweet perfume flowers everywhere, a white-gloved tea service was provided and, as Christmas was approaching, I was presented with an appetising, unfamiliar sweet dish called stollen cake smothered in fresh cream. Meanwhile, my father opted for Viennese pastries. In the opposite corner, violins gently played. 'Mmmm,' I thought. 'I am in Heaven.' The luxurious food was simply superb.

Next, we wandered up on deck for a breath of fresh air and a last look over the docks prior to disembarking. On deck, a German 'oompah' band

A dramatic view of the TS *Bremen* taken from a tug as she slowly sails past. (William Paulus)

was playing traditional foot-stomping music for passengers and visitors to the ship. My father explained that the ship had a long and distinguished history, being built as a French liner for the Sud Atlantique, before being managed by Cunard on behalf of the British Government during the Second World War. Thereafter it was returned to the French as a troopship and later sold to the North German Lloyd. My father commented that one day I might like to find out more about the ship, and this comment stuck in my mind. As a souvenir of our visit, my father was presented with a small bottle of German Pilsner beer with a label showing the ship on it. This bottle remained intact for many years, resting above on father's old mantelpiece at home until lost in a house move.

My lasting impression was that of a very happy Christmas atmosphere on the *Bremen,* which mere words find hard to describe. The German crew were a warm and friendly team who strived for perfection and achieved it.

As the golden age of transatlantic liners came to an end, the TS *Bremen* was sold to the Greek-owned Chandris Cruises and renamed *Regina Magna.* I rarely saw her at Southampton in her new form and only recall a passing glimpse from a Red Funnel Isle of Wight ferry. After a few short years, she was taken to Saudi Arabia to be used as an accommodation vessel. Here, she was neglected and became run-down to the point where the ship was sold for scrapping in Taiwan. I learned that en-route to the breakers she had rolled over and sunk in less than a minute. This news greatly shocked and saddened me, but I was glad that the liner I loved had escaped the humiliating fate of being cut up for a million razor blades!

Decades have now passed, but I have not forgotten this wonderful ocean liner and cruise ship. During a television filming interview with the German ZDF Television in Southampton, the conversation somehow touched on the former German flagship TS *Bremen.* The question was asked if I would consider writing a book about the liner. Without hesitation, I replied, yes. True to my late father's challenge, all those years earlier, I set out to discover more about the TS *Bremen*'s history. With the valuable assistance of my wife Annette, who is a French and German speaker, what I found out about her previous life as the French *Pasteur* and as a British Cunard-managed troopship is almost unbelievable. Here, then, is her story.

She was designed with the intention of being the most opulent and sporty way to cross the South Atlantic. Her once plush interiors would instead reverberate to the sound of heavy military boots; the fragrance of exquisite expensive French perfumes would give way to the pervasive smell of sweat and cordite.

Patriotically hailed by the French as theirs, *Pasteur,* the liner built for the Europe–South America service for the Sud Atlantique Line, was in post-war years to become their national troopship, being decorated twice by the nation. The British declared that she was the Cunard-administered troopship HMT *Pasteur,* with the large smoky funnel that helped win the Second World War. The German nation proudly claimed this classic liner as the North German Lloyd TS *Bremen,* their last German flagship. The Greeks asserted that the ship was the Chandris Line flagship and cruise ship, *Regina Magna.* To the Saudi Arabians the ship was their accommodation ship, *Saudi Phil I,* based at Jeddah, which they in turn sold to Philsimport International, who renamed her *Filipinas Saudi I.* Without doubt, this ship has one of the most interesting and illustrious careers in ocean liner history, being registered under six different national flags with five different names.

Her unique history is full of exciting action and adventure: escaping the fall of France to Canada with the French gold reserves, managing to avoid be scuttled, threatened by torpedoing from German U-boats, bombing by the Luftwaffe, outrunning a German surface raider, an attempted mutiny by German POWs and sinking in storms and gigantic waves in the Atlantic, miraculous resurrection from beneath a 10-storey-high rogue killer wave off the south-east African coast, and the discovery on the ship after the war of a precious treasure of France which had lain hidden for the duration of the war – to list but a few! She was acclaimed to be one of the safest liners ever built, yet her demise would take all of 50 seconds. This book tells the story of this great classic liner and war hero from beginning to end.

1

Compagnie de Navigation Sud Atlantique SS Pasteur
1938–40

Code identification: FNDC
(Tricolour French flag registered at Bordeaux.)
29,253 gross tonnage

Construction

The origins of the ship can be traced back to the inter-war years when there was fierce competition for passenger trade between Europe and South America. The Germans established the rivalry with their 27,561 ton Hamburg–South America Line luxury liner *Cap Arcona* of 1927. The Italians followed with the Navigazione Generale Italiana Line's MS *Augustus*, which was launched by Edda Mussolini, the daughter of the Italian dictator, Benito Mussolini. The new Italian liner was fitted out and made her maiden voyage on 10 November 1927 and they boasted that she could reach South America from Italy in 5 days with a cruising speed of 22 knots. Meanwhile, the British Royal Mail Packet Company converted the *Alcantara* and *Asturias* to steam propulsion in 1934 and thereby increased their speed to 19 knots.

The French responded to the challenge in 1931 with the Sud Atlantique's 42,512 ton, *L'Atlantique.* At 744ft in length, she was the biggest and most luxurious ship to operate the South American service. After 15 months service, disaster struck and she was lost in the Channel on 4 January 1933 following a devastating fire. The French did not give up their challenge on the South American service between Bordeaux and the River Plate, and

ordered a new vessel to replace their tragic loss. The contract for the new ship was signed for construction by Penhoet at the Chantiers et Ateliers de St Nazaire in yard number R8, and her name was to be *Pasteur*, after the famous scientist Louis Pasteur.

The new French ship was designed to be 29,253 tons, some 12,000 tons lighter than the *L'Atlantique* and 49ft shorter in length with an overall length of 696ft 10in. However, the new French ship was to be considerably faster in order to rival the British Royal Mail Company's new 25,688-ton liner, *Andes.* The load draft of 31ft 6in for the new *Pasteur* was limited by the depth of the muddy water in the estuary of the Argentinean River Plate at Buenos Aires.

The SS *Pasteur* under construction at Chantiers de l'Atlantique in St Nazaire in 1937. (William Paulus Collection)

The SS *Pasteur* under construction at Chantiers de l'Atlantique in St Nazaire in 1937. (William Paulus Collection)

An unusual view of the construction SS *Pasteur* at Chantiers de l'Atlantique in St Nazaire in 1937 showing the keel, prop shafts and rudder casing. The massive hull is supported by timber props. (Britton Collection)

On 15 February 1938, the *Pasteur* was launched by Madame Pasteur Vallery-Radot, wife of the grandson of Louis Pasteur. Although sometimes referred to as 'SS' (steam ship), it really was a 'TSS' (turbine steam ship). From the very beginning this ship as always be known and addressed by the French as 'He'.

The planned maiden voyage was delayed by the outbreak of fire while being fitted out, so the ship's maiden voyage from Bordeaux to Buenos Aires was rescheduled for 10 September 1939. The fire broke out on 9 March 1939 and started within the funnel as painting operations were underway. The wet paint spread the blaze and wooden scaffolding caught fire. Burning wood fell into the boiler room close to the fuel tanks, which were full to capacity. As the fire began to take hold, firemen poured huge volumes of water down the funnel, as the foam safety system had not been installed on the ship.

When the fire was extinguished, the smouldering, black, charred remains were examined to reveal that the fire, heat and salt water had caused extensive damage, with much of the new machinery being written off beyond economic repair. Some machinery was salvaged, removed for repair and cleaned. The consequence was that plans to make her ready for June had to be postponed until late July. However, completion and signing off was done in mid August and, following boiler and dock trials, the ship sailed from the yard on 19 August for trials in the Channel. The trials demonstrated that *Pasteur* could sustain 25½ knots quite easily and that 26 knots was achievable, although the vessel machinery was 'tight' in places and required thorough running in. Reports of the trials also highlight a few 'blown' boiler tubes for replacement.

Four sets of Parsons-type turbines drove the quadruple screw propellers through single reduction gearing at 200rpm. To power this, ten Penhoet water tube boilers worked at 441lbs psi and 385 degrees superheat. All the boilers discharged smoke emissions into the enormous funnel. Three 220-volt turbo generators were carried and two emergency generators. A ready supply of 200 tons of fresh water per day was provided by the two large evaporators.

The new *Pasteur* had nine decks: the bridge deck or upper boat deck; the sports deck, which was out to the side under the bridge deck, and, abaft that, the top of the deckhouse on A deck. Then came A deck, which extended from the fore end of the superstructure almost to the after derrick posts. B deck was the forecastle deck and below were C, D, E, and F decks, which ran the full length of the ship, and G deck was for outside machinery spaces. D deck was a bulkhead deck, while B deck formed the

Above: Incredible rivet detail on the port–side bow of the SS *Pasteur* showing her name and anchor whilst under construction at Chantiers de l'Atlantique in St Nazaire in 1937. (William Paulus Collection)

Above: The French tricolour flag flies proudly from the stern of the hull of the SS *Pasteur* whilst under construction at Chantiers de l'Atlantique in St Nazaire in 1937. The name, Pasteur, and home port, Bordeaux are embossed on the stern of the ship. (William Paulus Collection)

Right: The hull of the SS *Pasteur* appears to be nearing completion on the slipway at Chantiers de l'Atlantique in St Nazaire in January 1938. (Britton Collection)

The fitting out of the *Pasteur* is nearing completion with the external painting finished in late July 1939. (William Paulus Collection)

upper flange of the hull girder. Above B deck, the superstructure of the ship projected out 15in over the vessel's sides.

The sports deck had a very large club room forward, with a bar and games space, large ship's side windows and a covered promenade. Aft were a full-sized floodlit tennis court (described in company brochures as the 'realm of the young'), a ventilation machinery house and a sunbathing space. On A deck were the deck officer's rooms to port, stewards' rooms to starboard, a number of First Class rooms with private balconies, the upper half of the First Class saloon, engineer's quarters and a children's dining and playrooms. On B deck were the principal public rooms, lounge, saloon with seating for 256, restaurant, smoking room, veranda café, swimming pool and a Second Class promenade. On the deck below were the Third Class hall and promenade, First Class staterooms, galleys, bakeries and Second Class saloon and public rooms. D deck was given over to Third Class forward, and First Class Rooms were on F deck.

On 15 February 1938, the *Pasteur* was launched by Madame Pasteur Vallery–Radot, wife of the grandson of Louis Pasteur. Crowds of cheering well–wishers and shipyard workers watch as the hull of the new ship slides into the water at speed. (Britton Collection)

Captain Petiot is pictured on the bridge of the completed *Pasteur*, ready to take her to sea in August 1939. (Britton Collection)

Members of the French press board the *Pasteur* in 1939 for the sea trials. (Britton Collection

The bust of the French scientist Louis Pasteur, whom the ship is named after, on the *Pasteur* in August 1939. (Britton Collection)

The bridge of the completed *Pasteur*, with the crew about to take her to sea in August 1939. (Britton Collection)

A view of the engine room of the completed *Pasteur*, awaiting the order for 'slow ahead' to take her to sea in August 1939. (Britton Collection)

All fittings, fixtures and decoration in the First Class section were on a magnificent luxurious scale by the foremost French artists and designers of the day. Walls and ceilings were adorned with ornate plasterwork and original oil and watercolour paintings. Under foot, there were specially commissioned plush Balsan carpets from Chateauroux. The main salon was a peaceful room, oval in shape, with an impressive domed ceiling and tall windows, which opened onto the promenade deck. The walls and columns were set in a natural Chinese red by the designers, Dunand and Charpentier.

On the other side of the salon, moving aft, were the library and writing room, through which passengers passed into the compact main staircase. Here, stood a superb sculpture bust of Louis Pasteur by Real de Sarte. Double doors led to the most impressive room on board the ship, the First Class dining salon. This very large room gave passengers the impression of a fantastically beautiful undersea palace, with green oxidised copper wall coverings and gold-wrought iron filigree screens over the large windows. At the forward end of the room stood a magnificent sculpture entitled Diana and Stag, and at the aft end was an elaborate multilevel buffet. A short distance aft of the main dining salon was a private restaurant with thirty seats. The chairs in this intimate room were sycamore covered in Moroccan leather.

Heating and ventilation aboard were on the Thermotank system. Throughout the ship a comprehensive fire detection and extinction system was fitted with fireproof bullheads. Below decks, a foam system protected the engine and boiler rooms, CO_2 the cargo spaces, and steam the fuel tanks. All flammable materials on board were, in theory, 'reduced to a minimum'.

LE SALON

Top right: An artist's impression of the first-class lounge on the *Pasteur*. (Britton Collection)

Centre right: An artist's impression of the first-class lounge on the *Pasteur*. (Britton Collection)

Bottom right: This is an artist's impression of the SS *Pasteur's* first-class lounge and smoking room. Of interest on the immense mahogany pillars is the hand-carved inlaid map which depicts the path of the intended regular voyages across the South Atlantic. It is said that this room was one of the most attractive afloat, rivalling even the Cunard Queen liners. Deep club chairs with blue and white fern-patterned upholstery floated on a sea of midnight blue wall-to-wall carpeting. The whole ambiance of sheer luxury in this room was completed by a series of zodiac symbols and nautical themes by the renowned French artist Le Bourgeots. (Britton Collection)

An artist's impression of the *Pasteur* interior, 1939. (Britton Collection)

Pasteur interior, 1939. (Britton Collection)

Pasteur interior, 1939. (Britton Collection)

The eleven bulkheads on the *Pasteur* provided a two-compartment standard and divided the liner up into twelve compartments: the two peaks, two holds forward, oil fuel tank space, three boiler rooms, two engine rooms and two cargo and garage spaces aft. The forty-seven watertight doors in these bulkheads were hydraulically operated.

The two forward holds were for cargo, and the two spaces aft were also for cargo. The between decks space formed two large garages with 56,000cu.ft of space that were sectioned off by a watertight door. Two 4-ton cranes were provided right aft to lift vehicles on and off the ship. Two additional 3-ton cranes were located aft and two at No. 2 hatchway for the loading of cargo and stores.

Amidships on D and E Decks there was 24,000cu.ft of refrigerated spaces in lockers. The *Pasteur* had bow anchors which weighed 7½ tons each, and a stern anchor weighing 5½ tons. The ship was equipped with sixteen wooden lifeboats which could carry 88 persons each, two 30ft wooden motor boats and two 22ft wooden boats. There was also buoyancy apparatus for 352 persons.

A ship that carried the name of France's greatest medical scientist, Louis Pasteur, had to have state-of-the-art medical facilities, including two hospitals – one forward on C Deck and the other aft on D Deck. Facilities on C Deck included an operating room, consulting room, a small pharmacy and a convalescent room. The D Deck facility was for infectious

Pasteur library, 1939. (Britton Collection)

Pasteur children's playroom, 1939. (Britton Collection)

Pasteur first–class cabin, 1939. (Britton Collection)

Pasteur's chapel. (Britton Collection)

Pasteur second–class cabin, 1939. (Britton Collection)

Pasteur tourist-class cabin, 1939. (Britton Collection)

diseases. The ship carried three doctors, French, Spanish and Portuguese, all accommodated in separate cabins near the first-class embarkation hall and near to a consulting room.

Maiden Voyage and Second World War Service 1939–40

Although the *Pasteur* was never to make a commercial voyage, she did carry members of the press and invited guests on one occasion. Three hundred special guests of the Sud Atlantique Board came aboard the sparkling new ocean liner in Le Havre on Saturday, 19 August 1939, for a three-day-long cruise along the English coast. Sailing from Le Havre at 6 p.m., against the setting summer sun, the *Pasteur* is said to have looked very impressive as her enormous golden-yellow and black funnel was illuminated. That evening there was a special gala dinner for guests and members of the press. Passengers were said to be very impressed with the high standards and luxury aboard, but this was a one-off peacetime voyage as a dark shadow was to cast itself over Europe.

Events in Europe were to have a dramatic impact on the new *Pasteur*. On 30 August 1939, it was announced in the press that the commissioning ceremony for the *Pasteur*, scheduled for 9 September, had been cancelled indefinitely due to the international situation. When Germany invaded Poland on 1 September, followed by the declaration of war by Britain and France on 3 September, the maiden voyage was cancelled. There were threatening rumours that a German surface raider had secretly slipped out unnoticed into the Atlantic and was heading south. This rumour turned out to be true, as the German surface raider was none other than the pocket battleship *Admiral Graf Spee*, which was officially classified as a Deutschland Class heavy cruiser. When war broke out the *Pasteur* was in Brest following her sea trials. The directors of the Sud Atlantique met to discuss the proposed maiden voyage, and after a considered debate it was decided that there was too great a risk of losing their new asset, and the decision was made to return the *Pasteur* to St Nazaire. The French Government then served notice that the new liner was to be requisitioned. Whilst the *Pasteur* was laid up at St Nazaire, it was decided to remove all the new silverware, china and paintings and place them in storage.

The *Pasteur* remained at berth under guard in St Nazaire during the 'Phoney War' of 1939, but on 10 May 1940 devastating news came

The *Pasteur* setting out on her sea trials in 1939. (William Paulus Collection)

The *Pasteur* anchored off Bordeaux in 1939. (William Paulus Collection)

that the Germans were breaking through the French fortified Maginot Line with an offensive at the Ardennes. Panic began to spread as French forces collapsed in the face of blitzkrieg air bombing and rapid tank advancement. Consideration was now given for the future of the new *Pasteur* and instructions were issued to remove passenger fittings, paint her in a grey livery and fit her with eight basic gun pits equipped with 0.40-calibre machine guns abreast of the chartroom, funnel and mainmast, with guns fore and aft, and a 5in cannon, ready for her return to Brest on 1 June 1940.

Prior to the outbreak of war, the French Government gave serious consideration to the future welfare of their 2,340 tons gold reserves. Pierre Fournier, President of the Banque de France, proposed a plan, code named Macaroni, which outlined the transfer of the gold reserves to another country for safekeeping. After much deliberation, the plan was secretly

This is a large A1–sized black–and–white advert promoting Les Cafés du Bresil and the South American service of the Pasteur. (Britton Collection)

This is the *New York Times* actual press photo announcing the arrival of the *Pasteur* at New York on 11 June 1940. (Associated Press/ Britton Collection)

The SS *Pasteur* docking after arrival at New York on 11 June 1940, assisted by three tugs. (Ernest Arroyo Collection)

Early on the morning of 1 June, Frigate Captain Plesis, a representative of the French Government, came aboard the *Pasteur*. The crew of the ship were ordered to remain on board and the *Pasteur's* Captain Petiot was informed that he was going to be entrusted with an 'exceptional load of cargo' which would make him the richest man in the world for a short time. The *Pasteur* had been commissioned to carry the remaining French gold reserves for safety to Canada.

During the early hours of 1 June, heavily guarded covered lorries arrived at the quayside. More than 206 tons (210 metric tonnes) of gold reserves in the form of 10 and 20 franc gold coins, contained in 3,700 jute sacks arrived from the Banque de France and were quickly loaded aboard. The crew of the ship alone transferred the loads via the rear No. 2 crane into the hold. They were watched by Captain Plessis, twelve armed guards and Monsieur Poissonnier, who was representing the Bank. Loading commenced at 10 a.m. and was completed at 7 p.m. However, the material of fifty of the jute sacks was discovered to be rotten owing to age. Consequently, new sacks were made up from material on board and the rotten sacks were carefully placed straight into the new sacks. They were then sealed and stamped with a special matrix cobbled together on the ship.

adopted and French warships commenced the transfer of gold across the Atlantic to Halifax, Nova Scotia.

Under a strict veil of secrecy and total security, preparations were made on 29 May to reactivate the mothballed *Pasteur* and steam up her boilers.

In the evening of 1 June, Captain Francois Petiot learned orally that his secret destination was Halifax in Canada. Why Halifax, Canada? The answer was that the French Government required the gold reserves to be away from Europe and initially delivered to the safekeeping of the Royal Bank of Canada in Ottowa. It was the intention that the gold reserves would eventually be taken to New York, but it was arranged to transport them from Halifax via Ottowa by a land route.

Under the cover of darkness, in the early hours of 1 June, a British Royal Navy destroyer carrying members of the Royal Navy Volunteer Reserve, based at the Thornycroft Shipyard in Southampton, was dispatched to Brest with secret orders regarding the *Pasteur*. When at sea, the British forces were ordered to be taken to the *Pasteur* and were to assist the French crew with preparations for sailing. In the event of failure to make her ready to sail, the British forces were ordered to scuttle the ship across the harbour entrance! Fortunately, the boilers were warm and steam pressure built up, with all machinery responding well when checked.

On 2 June, unannounced, the *Pasteur* with 272 crew on board quietly slipped her moorings and headed out unlit, escorted by naval vessels at first into the English Channel. Once underway speed was increased to 26½ knots following a zigzag course and the British naval ratings on board expected the *Pasteur* to make towards Southampton, but Captain Marc Petiot opened his sealed orders and found written confirmation to sail across the Atlantic to Halifax, Nova Scotia, Canada.

According to the late Robert M. Johnston, RNVR Engineer on the *Pasteur,* the secret maiden voyage did not pass without incident. Bad weather caused the French escort ships to break off and leave the *Pasteur* to continue her voyage alone and at speed. Two days out, seawater contaminated the condenser loop in the *Pasteur's* boiler room and she was nervously halted at sea. The vessel perilously floated silently on the Atlantic waves so as not to attract lurking menacing German U-boats. Suddenly, loud bangs echoed across the stricken ship from the boiler room, as engineers toiled to quickly make repairs with a sledge hammer. A cold sweat shuddered down the spines of the crew as they anxiously waited on lookout. With mid-Atlantic condenser repairs successfully completed, the voyage recommenced and a tot of French cognac was dispatched to all members of the skeleton crew on board the *Pasteur*. On 5 June, the *Pasteur* passed the French cruiser *Emile Bertin* heading in the opposite direction returning empty following the first part of the delivery of the French gold reserves. For the remainder of the voyage, the *Pasteur* proved to be a fast ship, but there was some concern about the black smoke emissions from her large funnel, which potentially could alert the enemy beneath the waves peering through their periscopes. With great relief the ship eventually arrived in Halifax on 7 June.

The *Pasteur* remained under close guard and a blanket of security as the gold in the sacks was carefully unloaded on 8–9 June under the supervision of the Royal Canadian Mounted Police. The captain of the French Navy cruiser *Joan d'Arc* offered the assistance of members of his crew to help unload the sacks of gold from the *Pasteur,* but this was refused by Captain Petiot. No strangers or non-crew members of the *Pasteur* came in to contact with the handling of the gold sacks until they were handed over to the Canadians. With the task complete, the *Pasteur* set sail for New York on 9 June.

Entering unannounced in the neutral port of New York on 11 June 1940, first word of the new French ship arriving at Sandy Hook reached the press at 7.28 a.m. After leaving quarantine at 9 a.m., the *Pasteur* solemnly sailed through the early summer haze up the Hudson River and was berthed on the south side of Pier 88 alongside the magnificent three-funnel French flagship *Normandie*, under guard. During 13 June, external bridges were fitted at Todds Ship Yard and the ship took delivery of: forty-five crates of artillery shells, 263 coupling units bound for Dakar, 95–75mm canon shells and two former French 90mm canons built at St Etienne in 1892 acquired by the US Army in 1917–18. These canons were mounted on a petticoat gun carriage, but minus their gunsights. All this equipment was purchased by the French in May and June 1940. Documentation states that ten training planes were fitted on the sports deck. The provision of such ancient canons on the *Pasteur* left it under-gunned compared to other large former ocean liners on troopship duties, as they were equipped with larger 138mm guns.

On 14 June, devastating news reached the *Pasteur* that Paris had fallen, and just eight days later France surrendered. Following an exchange of telegrams between the French Naval Attaché in Washington and Captain Plessey on the ship, urgent orders were received that the *Pasteur* should be returned immediately to Halifax and she set sail on 17 June, arriving at Halifax at 10 p.m.

2

His Majesty's Transportship (HMT) Pasteur, British Government under Cunard White Star Management 1940–46

His Majesty's Admiralty number: 166306
Code letters: GNDW
(Sailing under the Blue Ensign British flag and registered at Liverpool.)

When news of the French Government signing the Armistice with Germany arrived on 22 June 1940, there was a feeling of utter despair and bewilderment by those on board the *Pasteur*. What would happen to them and their ship now? Canadian authorities boarded the ship, which was anchored in Bedford Basin off Halifax, at 8 a.m. on the morning of 4 July 1940 and formally requisitioned the *Pasteur* for the British. Some members of the French crew attempted to scuttle their ship, but were deterred from doing so by armed Canadian forces. *Pasteur* would now be manned by a mixed British and Canadian crew, flying the Blue Ensign British flag and placed under Cunard White Star Line management on behalf of the British Ministry of War. She was renamed HMT *Pasteur* and a traditional Cunard foolscap-sized card-bound captain's logbook was issued for future records of voyages. Along with the requisitioned Cunard RMS *Queen Mary*, RMS *Queen Elizabeth*, RMS *Mauretania*, Holland America Line SS *Nieuw Amsterdam* and French SS *Ile de France*, the *Pasteur* was to become part of a group of troop transport liners known as 'The Seven Seas Monsters'. Each of these former liners had a bounty of DM1 million on their head to be awarded by the German Führer Adolf Hitler to the successful German U-boat captain that sank them! As a gallant gesture, Cunard management in Liverpool directed that the *Pasteur* was to fly the French Tricolour on her foremast.

Back in Halifax, the grim-faced French crew of the *Pasteur* were evicted from the ship and sent by train to New York. Here they boarded the Greek Line ship, *Nea Hellas*, along with the crew from the French freighter *St Malo*, which was also in Halifax at the time. There was some resistance from the Greek crew to accept the French seamen, but they eventually sailed from New York on 17 July bound for Lisbon in Portugal, from where the French crews returned overland to their homes in France.

The HMT *Pasteur* remained at anchor in Halifax crewed by armed Canadian forces and by a few members of the Royal Navy Volunteer Reserve. Early in the morning of Thursday, 16 August, the first elements of the British Cunard skeleton crew, formerly on the new Cunard RMS *Queen Elizabeth*, arrived at Halifax from New York. The French crews had not made their successor's task any easier as they had hidden the plans for the *Pasteur* behind panels in the bulkheads! After a preliminary inspection by the Chief Engineer, it was noticed that the doors had been removed from eight of the ten boilers. The fireboxes and boilers were very dirty both inside and externally, so much so that a local Canadian specialist boiler subcontractor was summoned at short notice to clean them. There was great concern expressed by the British crew about the boiler feeds, and the boiler tubes were discovered to be rusted. On the plus side, the turbines were inspected and found to be in a satisfactory condition.

All essential repairs to the *Pasteur* were completed by 21 August, the boilers were lit and the ship was made ready to sail the following day, following a dock trial test of the engines and boilers. The *Pasteur* was given a new recognition call code, GKYL. With the assistance of a French-speaking Canadian interpreter, the ship sailed on 23 August for a

Left: A Royal Navy Able Seaman, complete with his helmet, rucksack and hammock, looks up at his new ship the HMT *Pasteur* at Halifax, Canada, on 4 July 1940. British crews boarded the ship on this day following requisition by the British Ministry of Defence. (William Paulus Collection)

'shake down' trial voyage to test compasses and the full working of the ship in order familiarise the crew. The propellers were worked at 160rpm, which was considered 'adequate' for the condition of the ship.

Mr W. Suttcliffe, the chief engineer, gave the 'all clear' for orders to sail on Sunday 25 August 1940 at midday. However, this order was cancelled with a postponement for sailing until Tuesday, 27 August. On 18 August, 1,954 tons of oil was pumped aboard, which topped up the oil tanks to a total of 6,326 tons. A total of 245 tons of oil were consumed on the dock trials and shake-down familiarisation voyage, which meant that 6,081 tons remained for the future voyage, which was considered sufficient.

The new British skeleton crew were considered to be 'under strength' and not effective, but after taking on board elements of troops from the Calgary Highlanders, the *Pasteur* sailed at 2.13 p.m. on 27 August

in the afternoon, bound for Gourock. She joined a convoy with two other ex-Cunard ships 19,730-ton RMS *Scythia* and the 19,695-ton RMS *Laconia*. The *Laconia* was later tragically torpedoed and sunk on 12 September 1942.

The convoy sailed very slowly at an average speed of just 15.29 knots, arriving at Gourock in 7 days 11 hours 47 minutes at 6 a.m. on the morning of 4 September. It was escorted by two British destroyers. The day before arriving, German U-boats were detected off the north-west coast of Ireland seeking to target the convoy. During the hours of darkness, the destroyer escorts broke off and commenced depth charging their submerged foe. The underwater explosions were so close to the hull of the *Pasteur* that damage was caused to the port-side lubricators and feed pump. The feed pump stopped working altogether, causing overheating.

After safely disembarking the Calgary Highlander troops, the *Pasteur* continued to her destination at Liverpool, sailing from Gourock at 8.19 p.m. on the evening of 5 September and arriving the next morning at Liverpool Bar at 7.57 a.m. Unfortunately, she arrived in Liverpool just as Heinkel and Dornier aircraft of German Luftwaffe were commencing a bombing raid on the Chemical Company in Norfolk Street and Milner Safe Works in Smithdown Lane, which killed ten people. The navigator of a Dornier aircraft spotted the inky black smoke from the funnel of the *Pasteur* and immediately alerted members of his squadron to brake off and target the troopship. The *Pasteur* now became the primary target for the German Luftwaffe aircraft with any remaining bombs. Bombs rained down from the sky and the ship tried her best to zigzag her course to avoid the bombs. Bombs detonated all around the ship, but not one hit the target. The explosions, however, did cause damage to the starboard-side dynamo, which stopped and had to be replaced by a back-up dynamo. Several hours after the raid, a fractured valve in the feed pump was also detected, as a result of the air raid, but it was a baptism-of-fire welcome to Liverpool for the *Pasteur*.

A new ship's master took command of the *Pasteur* at midday on 6 September, Captain R.H. Murchie, who was to stay in command of the ship until the end of 1941. The new captain identified that the major problem with the management of the *Pasteur* was that everything was marked in French, including signs, labels, instructions, working diagrams and plans. This was partially overcome by the assistance of Canadian Navy ratings acting as interpreters. Upon docking in Liverpool, Cunard and the Admiralty had revised documentation, plans and working diagrams for the *Pasteur* redrafted into English. In the meantime, as the attached correspondence

Above: Wartime logbooks.

from J. Austin, superintendent engineer of Cunard White Star Line, revealed considerable work had to be undertaken to the ship's boilers and mechanical operating gear to make the ship fully seaworthy and convert her into a troopship. Cabins were radically transformed with removal of fixtures and fittings to be replaced by simple bunk beds to increase capacity. The interior of the *Pasteur* was almost totally unrecognisable, except for a few rooms designated for the captain and officers.

After emerging from her Liverpool intermediate refit, some of the initial problems had been resolved. The introduction of Manchester-built Davies & Metcalfe lubricators with drip feeds coupled to oil reservoirs revolutionised the working machinery. Similarly, regular sprinklings in fireboxes of sand to clear the tubes improved steam qualities of the French boilers. Unfortunately, this had a side effect of creating visible black smoke at sea. Four sets of Parsons-type turbines could now drive the quadruple screw propellers of the *Pasteur* at a full 200rpm through single reduction gearing, instead of the 180rpm restriction when the ship was taken over at Halifax. Each set consisted of an h.p. impulse ahead turbine, an l.p. reaction ahead turbine with impulse astern blading, and an l.p. ahead impulse turbine. Michell thrust blocks were fitted throughout. This renovated machinery developed 62,000shp, and although initially designed for a speed of 25 knots the new British Cunard troopship was now capable of achieving 26 knots cruising speed for sustained long distances, with a top burst of speed of 29 knots over a limited distance in calm seas, if required.

Several Cunard staff who were in Liverpool in September 1940 openly expressed their feeling towards the French-built *Pasteur*. Geoffrey Thrippleton Marr (later Commodore Marr DSC, RD, last Master of the Cunard RMS *Queen Elizabeth*), related:

When the *Pasteur* arrived in Liverpool what first caught my eye was her enormous funnel. I was later to discover that this acted like a gigantic sail and with her light draft she would have a tendency to pitch and roll. Although a fast ship, my reaction was that the French design was not pleasing or nicely proportioned, compared to our British John Brown-built Cunard *Mauretania*, of the same era. During a visit at Liverpool aboard the *Pasteur*, my observation was that the ship appeared to be rusting in places, shabby and run-down. Chatting to the British Cunard engineering staff, they confirmed that she was leaking steam and there were major problems with the feeds. The metric measurement fittings were causing some difficulty and confusion to the British engineers as all our Cunard ships were built to Imperial measurement. The ship was full of local Liverpudlian Scouse fitters, painters and carpenters with a sprinkling of Scottish John Brown workers and some Jordie engineers from Swan Hunters at Newcastle. New British Imperial measurements doors were delivered to the ship to be fitted and of course did not match the frames. Consequently, there was much cutting and hammering to convert the *Pasteur* to conform to British standards. To a man throughout the ship they were all swearing and cursing the French metric boilers, machinery and door measurements! Welcome to the war I thought.

Cunard Staff Captain, the late Eric Ashton-Irvine, reminisced:

We received orders in New York from Cunard to leave the *Queen Elizabeth* and travel up to Halifax. I recall it was bitterly cold journey and by the time we arrived to take over the *Pasteur* the skeleton crew were very tied, cold and hungry. On arrival at Halifax, we were all searched and checked as Nazi sympathisers had actually tried to sink her. She was one of my least favourite ships and was not a good sea boat. She

rolled and pitched enormously, had a rather shallow draft and her huge funnel caused wind problems. Within, there were especially low ceilings and too many interconnecting cabins and glass-mirrored bathrooms which were confusing, to say the least. Below our engineers relied on Canadian ratings to interpret the French language controls. [It was] a totally unsatisfactory position and I was glad to step ashore at Liverpool.

On 7 September, after remedial repairs, the *Pasteur* was readied for a series of transatlantic voyages.

On entering Liverpool on 27 October, the *Pasteur* entered Huskisson Dock where Cammell Laird Shipyard staff were waiting to rapidly assist with refit, repair and full conversion and fitting out to a troopship. This included the installation of two 100mm anti-aircraft guns, one forward of the forecastle and one sited on the upper aft forecastle. Within the short space of 24 hours, working around the clock, the *Pasteur* remarkably left the dock due to the threat of Luftwaffe air attack.

The next day, 29 October, relief troops, RAF personal and Royal Navy marines and ratings embarked on the *Pasteur* destined for Gibraltar, via Greenock. The log records reveal that the voyage to Greenock was in gloomy autumnal weather, supported by two Coastal Command Avro Anson aircraft and accompanied by two Royal Navy destroyers. On 31 October the *Pasteur* sailed from the Clyde for Gibraltar escorted by the Royal Navy aircraft carrier HMS *Ark Royal*, cruiser HMS *Glasgow* and four destroyers. The convoy passed around the coast of Northern Ireland and met stormy conditions in the eastern Atlantic. The log records that four other escorts joined the convoy whilst sailing south, two on 2 November and two on 4 November. On arrival at Gibraltar on the evening of 6 November, the crew on the *Pasteur* were surprised to see that the naval base was fully illuminated and that lights twinkled like stars in the darkness along the African coastline in the south. The ship dropped anchor 50 yards from shore next to the neutral Spanish waters. Everyone remained on board, except for the relief military personal that were taken ashore by tender.

The records reveal that while remaining at anchor off Gibraltar aerial bombings could be heard on 8 November, but no aeroplanes could be seen as the *Pasteur* refuelled and took on fresh water and supplies. The next day, steam pressure was built up in the boilers of the *Pasteur* and the ship sailed from the Rock of Gibraltar, returning to Scotland at maximum speed following a zigzag pattern course in order to avoid enemy U-boats.

On arrival at Greenock, the ship embarked Royal Australian troops but did not sail and the rowdy and complaining Australians had to swiftly disembark again owing to mechanical problems on board the ship. The *Pasteur* limped back into Glasgow under tow for emergency repairs.

Following the completion of repairs, including some boiler tube replacement, on 21 November the *Pasteur* completed the embarkation of 1,000 airmen and RAF ground support staff. They are bound for Carberry, Canada, in order to form the first Canadian training base for RAF pilots and navigators. Many of these airmen would return to British shores in 1943, ready to engage the German Luftwaffe in the skies over Europe, North Africa and the Far East.

On 27 November, the *Pasteur* sailed from the Clyde at 3 a.m. in a convoy bound for Halifax, Canada, with Royal Navy escort ships and the 27,000-ton troopship *Capetown Castle*. Soon after sailing, just 80 miles to the west of the coast of Ireland, however, two of the *Pasteur*'s engines broke down. The *Pasteur* stopped and the stricken ship was left helpless and drifting on the Atlantic for three hours, while urgent repairs were affected. Not for the first time in the career of the *Pasteur,* the whole ship was placed in 'silence', except for the engineers below. Everyone sweated, anxiously watching the horizon and praying the presence of the *Pasteur* would remain undiscovered.

Through binoculars, the lookouts spotted lifeboats and debris from a wreck bobbing up and down on the waves. The question in everyone's mind was, 'Would they soon be joining them if the *Pasteur* was torpedoed?'

After what seemed three endless hours, one engine was eventually restored after repair at sea. The ship managed to continue at a much reduced speed with one engine only. On the nights of 27–29 November, the escort destroyers broke off from the convoy to engage and sink two German U-boats. In so doing, one of the escorts suffered damage through ramming a U-boat. The *Capetown Castle* remained close to the *Pasteur* for the remainder of the voyage. On 30 November, the *Pasteur* headed north, now on its own, to enter Halifax on 4 December. The entry into the port was very slow and cautious as there was ice in the sea and the coastline was veiled in a covering of white snow.

Between 6 and 14 December, the *Pasteur* was under repair at St John, New Brunswick, Canada, where engine repairs were carried out in dry dock.

After taking on Bunker C fuel oil, fresh water and supplies, the *Pasteur* set sail again on 16 November from Halifax to join up with the *Capetown Castle* again as part of Convoy TC 8 to sail to Liverpool. Sailing close to the *Pasteur* in the convoy was the former Holland America Line ship, the troopship HMT *Pennland*. This vessel was later bombed and sunk in the Bay of Athens on 25 February 1941. Convoy TC 8 also contained two other vessels and a special freighter packed with TNT explosives. A destroyer was provided by the Royal Navy as an escort but leading the convoy was the ancient Royal Navy battleship HMS *Royal Sovereign*. The presence of this capital ship, a veteran of the First World War Battle of Jutland, with its eight 15in guns, gave all those on board the *Pasteur* a great sense of security.

On 17 December, the weather in the Atlantic began to deteriorate, with strong storm-force winds and gigantic 40ft waves breaking over the *Pasteur*. The ship began to roll violently and there was great seasickness in those on board. In all this 'living Hell', the engines stopped. After the storm subsided, the *Pasteur* managed to restart her engines and resume her voyage. A signal received on 21 December led to the battleship HMS *Royal Sovereign* breaking off from the convoy, and the *Pasteur* was now designated as the senior command ship and leader of the convoy.

Early on 23 December, as most sailor's were looking forward to Christmas leave at home, disaster struck Convoy TC8 as the engines of the special freighter carrying TNT broke down. The captain of the *Capetown Castle* signalled that he did not wish to stop and the ship continued ahead. The *Pasteur* stopped engines to wait with the stricken freighter throughout darkness during the night. Looking through the binoculars, the lookouts on the *Pasteur* could just make out the *Capetown Castle*, 20 miles ahead, which was being bombed and machine-gunned by German aircraft. At first light, Captain Murchie on the *Pasteur* took the decision that it was too dangerous for the ship to linger any longer and he reluctantly sailed on.

The German Kriegsmarine Headquarters in Berlin was aware of the sailing of the *Pasteur* across the Atlantic and dispatched from Norway long-range Focke-Wulf Fw 200 Condor aircraft to seek out the troopship. Once the four-engined aircraft located the ship a signal was sent to all U-boats and they were alerted and the ship slowed down as the result of bombing and machine-gunning. In the earlier attack on the *Capetown Castle*, the Condor aircraft pilot incorrectly assumed it had located the *Pasteur*. The ship now increased speed to her maximum and, with much relief and cheering from those on board, she entered home waters on the Clyde on Christmas Eve. After disembarking those on board, the crew of the *Pasteur* were given much needed shore leave.

Due to her speed, the *Pasteur* generally made her troopship voyages alone, without escort, but on occasions she did make voyages as a member of a convoy. On other occasions, the *Pasteur* sailed at speed in tandem with her French running-mate ocean liner, the SS *Ile de France*. Between 1940 and 1943, a series of fast military convoys called the

'Winston Specials' or WS convoys, carried troops and equipment to the Middle East, India and occasionally to the Far East. The WS convoy series was replaced in August 1943 by the KMF convoy series which sailed to North African ports and eventually to Suez. Listed in the text below, outlining the war service of the *Pasteur*, are details relating to WS convoys in which she participated.

The WS convoy series sailed mainly from Liverpool and the Clyde, the two sections of the convoy joining south of Oversay in the Outer Hebrides. The combined convoy, often splitting to fast and slow groups, then sailed to: Freetown, Sierra Leone, before continuing to the Cape. Here the convoy usually split once more with one section stopping over in Capetown and the other in Durban. The convoy would once again reform off Durban before continuing onwards into the Indian Ocean. Here it would split again into the Suez section (usually designated 'A') and the Indian section to Bombay (designated 'B') and other destinations to the east such as Singapore and Bhutan.

1941

The *Pasteur* was recorded as entering dry dock at Greenock for an extensive refit until late March 1941. Reports indicate that there was a serious fire on board, but it is not clear if occurred during the refit or was the reason for the refit. There is a record of thirty-three sailors being transferred to the ship on 2 February, which indicates that the ship was being prepared for steaming and possible trials.

Reports filtered through to the crew of the *Pasteur* that the German cruisers *Scharnhorst* and *Gneisenau,* under the command of Admiral Lutjens, had returned to the French port of Brest on 22 March after a successful raid on shipping off Freetown, sinking a total of thirty-one merchant vessels. The two German surface killers had been supported by three Luftwaffe HE-115s (operating from France) and submarines U-105 and U-124. The Admiralty in Whitehall were uncertain of these German surface ships' future exploits, and there was a significant potential threat to the next southbound Convoy WS 7, of which *Pasteur* was to be a member.

On 23 March, the *Pasteur* loaded and made ready to join Convoy WS 7 which was transporting 80,000 troop reinforcements for the 8th Army in the North African campaign. Full details are set out here.

This is a very rare original photograph of the HMT *Pasteur* foredeck showing Free French Special Forces bound for North Africa in 1941. This secret photo was taken in the Indian Ocean and hidden for over 60 years! (Britton Collection)

Convoy WS 7

The convoy assembled in the Clyde anchorage and sailed from there on 24 March 1941 in the following formation:

11 DUCHESS OF YORK	21 STIRLING CASTLE (Vice Commodore)	31 DUCHESS OF ATHOLL	41 EMPRESS OF CANADA (Commodore)	51 WARWICK CASTLE	61 OTRANTO
12 VICEROY OF INDIA	22 DENBIGHSHIRE	32 ORION	42 STRATHEDEN	52 STRATHNAVER	62 ORCADES
13 ANDES	23 JOHAN VAN OLDENBARNEVELT	33 STRATHALLAN	43 **PASTEUR**	53 STRATHMORE	
14 GEORGIC	24 DEMPO	34 ORONTES	54 GLENORCHY		

Georgic detached to Halifax 28.3, *Strathaird* (not allocated a number in the plan above) was in collision with *Stirling Castle* shortly after sailing and obliged to return.

At a later stage, *Glenorchy* took position 63, retaining that thereafter.

A/S escorts for the convoy were supplied for the periods shown below by the destroyers.

Ocean escort was provided by the Royal Navy battleship HMS *Revenge* between 24 and 28 March; she then detached and escorted *Georgic* to Halifax, Nova Scotia. The battleship HMS *Nelson*, accompanied by the destroyer HMS *Arrow*, escorted the convoy to Freetown. The convoy stopped at Freetown from 4 to 7 April, taking on fresh water and fruit supplies.

Off Freetown, the destroyers HMS *Duncan* and HMS *Foxhound* joined on 1 April and HMS *Vidette* and HMS *Wishart,* from 2 April until arrival on 4 April.

The complete convoy sailed from Freetown on 7 April escorted by *Foxhound* to 8 April and *Duncan*, *Vidette* and *Wishart* to 9 April. *Nelson* provided ocean escort from 7 April until 15 April when she was relieved by the cruiser HMS *Newcastle* which escorted the convoy to Capetown, arriving 16 April, and then took the Durban ships on to that port, arriving 19 April, returning then to Simonstown.

Andes, Dempo, Duchess of Atholl, Duchess of York, Empress of Canada, Orcades, Orion, Pasteur, Strathallan, Stratheden and *Strathmore* entered Capetown, D*empo* sailing later the same day as an independent to Durban where she arrived 20 Apriil; the remaining ships went on to berth at Durban. The logbook records indicate that the *Pasteur* off loaded evacuees from the United Kingdom for transfer to Australia and New Zealand.

The *Pasteur* entered the Gulf of Aden on 1 May and arrived at Suez on 6 May, dropping anchor next to the Cunard RMS *Queen Elizabeth*, RMS *Queen Mary*, RMS *Mauretania*, SS *Ile de France,* and SS *Nieuw Amsterdam.* They were classified by the Allies under the codeword as '*Monsters*'. This super-fleet of *Monsters* was the greatest collection of liners ever assembled together in one place in the Second World War. On 7 May, the RMS *Queen Mary* sailed off alone to Australia.

The *Pasteur* sailed from Suez on 11 May, stopping off at Capetown (on 22 May), and Port of Spain, Trinidad, West Indies, before arriving at St Johns, New Brunswick, Canada, to enter dry dock in mid June. The entry into the dry dock was a very difficult maneuver, as the weather was thick fog. This fog lingered for some days and there is a record of fog when she

entered Halifax on 19 June before sailing to Liverpool on 21 June with the 117th US Army General Hospital Unit and Calgary Tank Regiment on board. On this voyage the *Pasteur* was part of Convoy TC11 which was made up of five other ships, escorted by the Renown class battlecruiser HMS *Repulse* (later sunk in a Japanese air attack in December 1941) and Revenge class battleship HMS *Ramilles,* plus eight destroyers.

The voyage across the North Atlantic was said to be treacherous, with 30 and 40ft waves crashing over the *Pasteur*, causing much seasickness for days! The convoy was relieved to eventually arrive at Liverpool on 29 June.

After unloading and refueling, the *Pasteur* was prepared to be part of '*Operation Substance*' for the resupply of the island of Malta. She was made ready to be part of Convoy WS 9C to travel as far as Gibraltar, where troops bound for Malta transferred to the *Leinster* and 4,200 troops specifically for Gibraltar.

Convoy WS 9C

Sailing from Newport (N), Swansea (S), Liverpool and the Clyde and assembling off Oversay on 13 July 1941, this convoy consisted principally of ships destined for Operation Substance, a supply convoy to Malta.

The convoy formation on sailing was:

11C HMS MANCHESTER	21C AVILA STAR	31C PASTEUR (Commodore)	41C MELBOURNE STAR (Vice Commodore)	51 HMS MANXMAN
12S DEUCALION	22C LEINSTER	32C HMS NELSON	42N DURHAM	52L CITY OF PRETORIA
13C HNETHMS HEEMSKERK	23N PORT CHALMERS	33L SYDNEY STAR		53C HMS ARETHUSA

The *Pasteur* had 4,200 troops embarked for the relief of the Gibraltar garrison.

The escort vessels were from the Bristol Channel:

The cruiser *Heemskerk* and the sloop *Stork* (the latter until 13 July). The Dutch AA cruiser *Heemskerk* and destroyers: HMS *Garland*, HMS *Gurkha*, HMS *Vanoc* and HMS *Wanderer* 12 to 15 July; battleship HMS *Nelson*, cruisers HMS *Manchester*, *Arethusa* and destroyers *Cossack*, *Lightning*, *Maori*, *Nestor* and *Sikh* 12 to 17 July. The cruiser HMS *Edinburgh* was in company on 20 July, the minelayer HMS *Manxman* from 15 to 16 July and the destroyer *Firedrake* joined from Gibraltar 18 July. The destroyer HMS *Winchelsea* also sailed with the convoy.

The *Pasteur* detached to Gibraltar 17 July, escorted by *Manchester*, *Lightning* and *Nestor* plus *Avon Vale*, *Eridge* and *Farndale* from Gibraltar; *Leinster* also detached that day with *Arethusa* plus *Cossack* and *Sikh*, while *Avila Star* detached as an independent on 16 July. All ships of the convoy destined for Gibraltar had arrived by 20 July 1941.

After the troops had left the *Pasteur* at Gibraltar, she continued forward to the Indian Ocean and Suez, before returning to Gornock on the 8 September. The ship unloaded, refueled and resupplied with provisions, ready to sail on 15 September for Halifax. Members of the RAF regiment and training crews boarded the *Pasteur* on 14 September, bound for air training schools in Canada and the USA.

In October 1941, the *Pasteur* made a voyage from Glasgow to Halifax with a varied complement including officers arranging the transport of 20,000 British troops across Canada and the Pacific to Singapore. She returned loaded with German prisoners of war destined for prison camps located in North America. Whilst in the Middle East, the *Pasteur* conveyed 2,000 German prisoners from Suez, Egypt to Durban in South Africa.

From Halifax the *Pasteur* docked in Quebec, for the first time in its career, on the 17 October. She returned to the United Kingdom on 5 November, carrying ninety-four postbags of mail. Again on this voyage, after four days, the ship encountered fierce Atlantic storms. The *Pasteur* is recorded as suffering very badly in this storm, with all unsecured fixtures and fittings violently and dangerously rolling around the decks. There is record of the fire extinguishers jumping out of their housings and uncontrollably spraying everything around them like a fountain. Similarly, in the officers' lounge a piano wildly broke loose and careered out of control across the floor. Pounding waves crashing over the ship plucked an Erlikon gun and a lifeboat from the deck. To compound all this, the passengers on board listening to the BBC radio had their programme interrupted by the Nazi propaganda programme, *Germany Calling*. They learned from Lord Haw Haw (William Joyce) that the ship they were travelling on had sunk, which was obviously a complete lie! Concerned friends and relatives were relieved when the *Pasteur* arrived safely at Gournock.

The ship sailed again on 23 November and arrived in Halifax on 1 December. Here the *Pasteur* was temporarily held, awaiting the arrival of the *Lord Rodney*, which was bound for the West Indies. As soon as the *Lord Rodney* arrived, passengers and equipment were transferred and the *Pasteur* continued her voyage to Montreal.

1942

From 1 January, a new ship's master, Captain Finlow, took command of the *Pasteur*. After familiarisation of the ship, the officers and crew, he prepared the *Pasteur* for a demanding voyage. The planned sailing of the *Pasteur* from Greenock on 8 January was delayed by 3–4 days owing to dense fog. The ship eventually sailed as part of the large Convoy WS 15 with secret orders to sail with reinforcements for the garrison of Singapore. On board the *Pasteur* were hundreds of young officers who were as yet not provided with orders or notification of their destination. It was a voyage, however, where dramatic developments in Singapore were to change the final destinations.

Singapore was a major military base and nicknamed the 'Gibraltar of the East'. It was unthinkable that this bastion of the British Empire would ever fall to the forces of Japan. News reached the ship that intensive fighting had commenced in Singapore on 8 February and then the unbelievable news was received that Lieutenant General Arthur Percival had surrendered to Japanese forces on 15 February. The news of the largest surrender of British-led forces in history was greeted with utter shock and disbelief by all those on board the *Pasteur* and the other ships in the convoy. So where next for the convoy? The answer was to divert to another theatre of war, North Africa.

Convoy WS 15

The convoy sailed from Liverpool (12 January 1942) and the Clyde (11 January 1942), and finally formed up off Oversay on 12 January 1942 in the formation shown here:

11C PORT CHALMERS	21L EMPIRE WOODLARK	31 HMS RESOLUTION	41C STRATHMORE (Commodore)	51C STAFFORDSHIRE	61C AUTOLYCUS	71C PARDO
12L MELBOURNE STAR	22L OTRANTO	32C HMS CHESHIRE	42C BRITANNIC	52C VICEROY OF INDIA	62C HNETHMS COLOMBIA	72C DORSET
13L ELISABETH BAKKE	23L ORONTES	33C HMS ASCANIA	43C LACONIA	53C STRATHNAVER (Vice Commodore)	63C CHRISTIAAN HUYGENS	73C LLANGIBBY CASTLE
24L ARAWA	34 HNETHMS HEEMSKERK	44C STIRLING CASTLE	54C PASTEUR	64L LETITIA	74C AAGTEKERK	

The escort force was made up of the destroyers shown below:

HMS *Vanoc* and HMS *Walker* 12 to 15 January, HMS *Vanquisher,* HMS *Volunteer* and Witherington 12 to 17 January, *Anthony* 17 to 18 January, Garland and N*orman* 17 to 25 January, V*ansIttart* and *Vimy* 21 to 25 January.

Ocean escort, other than as shown above, was provided by the armed merchant cruisers *Ascania* and *Cheshire*, the Dutch AA cruiser *Heemskerk* and the destroyer *Boreas* from 12 to 25 January, while the Royal Navy battleship *HMS Resolution* joined on 17 January to 25 January, the convoy arriving at Freetown 25 January 1942.

The first casualty for some time in WS convoys, and the first due to submarine attack, took place on 16 January when *Llangibby Castle* was hit right aft by a torpedo from the German U-boat U-402. She retired damaged to Ponta Delgada from where, under escort and accompanied by a tug, she returned to Gibraltar and then to Southampton for repairs.

A number of the warships listed as ocean escort were in fact en route to the Indian Ocean for duty; also included was the Turkish destroyer *Demir Hisar*, which was recently completed in Britain. She was temporarily commissioned with a British Royal Navy crew for the delivery voyage and operated as part of the escort.

The convoy sailed from Freetown on 29 January with its formation unchanged, escorted by the battleship *Resolution*, armed merchant cruiser *Cheshire* and destroyer *Demir Hisar* for Capetown, off which port it arrived on 9 February when *Dorset, Elisabeth Bakke, Laconia, Orontes* and *Pasteur* plus the Dutch submarine depot ship *Columbia* were detached to enter Capetown under escort of *Resolution*, arriving 10 February while the remainder of the convoy went on to Durban, arriving 13 February, accompanied by the armed merchant cruisers *Dunnottar Castle* and *Worcestershire* and the sloop *Milford*.

The five Capetown ships (the *Elisabeth Bakke* remained at Capetown) sailed 14 February escorted by the armed merchant cruiser HMS *Cheshire* and made their rendezvous with the Durban contingent (less *Arawa* and *Letita*) off that port on 17 February.

The escort from Durban consisted of the cruiser HMS *Ceres*, and the destroyer HMS *Norman* with the HMS *Cheshire* from Capetown.

During the northward passage, a three-part division of the convoy took place.

Convoy WS 15A

Dorset, Laconia, Melbourne Star, Orontes, Otranto, Pasteur and *Viceroy of India* detached on 26 February and were escorted to the vicinity of Aden by the cruisers HMS *Ceres* and HMS *Colombo*, dispersing off Aden 1 March 1942 to proceed independently to Suez.

The *Pasteur* arrived safely at Aden on 1 March before sailing on to Port Tewfik, arriving on 6 March.

The next voyage, sailing south from Suez, was also to prove very dramatic. Before sailing, the *Pasteur* was loaded with 140 tired and weary Royal Marines who were survivors of the sinking of HMS *Barham,* which had been torpedoed by a German U-boat on 25 November 1941 in the Mediterranean. Also coming aboard the *Pasteur* were 2,000 German prisoners of war captured in North Africa and bound for prison camps in South Africa. They were guarded by South African soldiers who spoke Afrikaans and could partially understand German. One of the South African sentries overheard some of the captured prisoners from a German U-boat crew plotting to attack the guards and forcibly seize the ship. The South African guard understood enough German to learn what was about to take place. He immediately reported the facts to his superior officer.

As the sun gently rose over the coast of East Africa, the crew of the *Pasteur* and Allied troops on board were aroused and armed with rifles. The German prisoners were awakened and escorted under close arms to the forward deck, where they were separated from their officers who were briskly marched to the after lounge. Crewmen and guards then searched the prisoner's quarters for weapons. Hidden were a mass of weapons including: strips of wood shaved from tables and stools, flattened out and sharpened forks and knives with points burnt to harden them. Some automatic pistols had somehow been secretly smuggled aboard! The potential mutiny on the *Pasteur* was a very close shave and had it not been for the actions of the resourceful and alert South African guard, the plotters may well have taken control of the *Pasteur*. News of the potential mutiny aboard the *Pasteur* was signalled ahead and a heavily armed reception awaited the arrival of the ship at Durban on 18 March. News film cameramen were waiting to record to German POWs disembark with Royal Marines equipped with machine guns carefully monitoring proceedings, watching for the mere sign of any trouble. Under the supervision of South African guards the German POWs quietly filed off the ship with dejected faces, accepting their fate in a prison camp.

The ship next sailed from Durban onwards to Capetown where she took on 2,000 tons of Bunker C fuel oil, supplies and fresh water, before returning to Egypt. Here the *Pasteur* embarked Italian POWs bound for Canada. Arrival in Canada was a great relief to all those onboard the ship for a much needed for rest and recuperation, while the *Pasteur* underwent refit. She emerged from refit re-equipped with facilities for the accommodation of 4,281 passengers of all ranks. However, this had come at the expense of forfeiting the space in the forward cargo hold. The fitting of a new radar system on the roof of the bridge on the starboard side was a new navigational aid to benefit the ship, which would be retained after the war. After refuelling, the *Pasteur* was made ready to join Convoy WS 19, details of which are listed here.

Convoy WS 19

This convoy assembled off Oversay on 10 May 1942 in the following formation:

11L LANARKSHIRE	21L MONARCH OF BERMUDA	31L MORETON BAY	41C STRATHNAVER (Commodore)	51C MOOLTAN	61A AKAROA
12L CLAN MACARTHUR	22L ORMONDE	32L SCYTHIA	42C STRATHAIRD	52C ORIZABA (Vice Commodore)	62A HIGHLAND MONARCH
23L HIGHLAND BRIGADE	33L ATHLONE CASTLE (Rear Commodore)	43C *PASTEUR*	53C BORINQUEN	63C SUSSEX	

The *Akaroa* detached as an independent for Bermuda on 14 May.

The escort ships comprised:

The Royal Navy destroyers *Keppel*, *Leamington* and *Volunteer* 10h to 13 May, *St Marys* 10 to 15 May and Castleton 10 to 16 May.

The cruiser HMS *Mauritius*, armed merchant cruiser *Carnarvon Castle* and destroyers *Belvoir* and *Hursley* escorted 11 to 22 May, while a local escort of the destroyers *Velox* on 19 May and *Boreas* and *Wild Swan* on 20 May joined from Freetown, where the convoy arrived on 22 May 1942.

Unusually, while still a Royal Navy vessel, *Carnarvon Castle* had 1,044 troops embarked for passage.

The convoy sailed from Freetown 26 May escorted by the destroyers HMS *Boreas* and *Velox* to 28 May, the armed merchant cruiser *Alcantara* 26 to 29 May, destroyer *Belvoir* 26 to 31 May while the cruiser *Mauritius*, destroyer *Hursley* and sloop *Milford* covered the whole passage from Freetown to Capetown where they convoy arrived on 5 June 1942. The cruiser HMS *Shropshire* joined off Capetown to escort the Durban ships to that port where they arrived 9 June 1942. *Highland Brigade*, which proceeded to the Plate, detached from the convoy 28 May to go to Takoradi, where she arrived on 31 May, later proceeding to South America.

Clan MacArthur, *Moreton Bay*, *Orizaba*, *Ormonde*, *Pasteur* and *Strathaird* went on to Durban, remaining ships entered Capetown.

The *Pasteur* next set sail from East Africa and headed to Washington, USA, with Italian POWs. At Freetown on 8 July, revised orders were received to proceed to New York. The next voyage was from 16 July to 16 August 1942, from New York to Port Tewfik, Egypt, sailing alone with 5,000 troops, consisting of US GIs of the 1st Army Corp, pilots and ground support crew from the 98th Aerial Bombing Group and soldiers from the 323 Service Group. The US troops on board were reinforcements for the North African Campaign. As they were the first US forces to participate in this theatre of the Second World War, they were accompanied by US Forces photographer James Hudson who, equipped with the latest Kodak colour film, recorded those onboard for posterity.

As the *Pasteur* sailed from New York down the Hudson River she was escorted by two destroyers. After passing the Statue of Liberty into the Narrows, the presence of a German U-boat was detected. Action stations was sounded and the crew manned their guns, while all troops gathered on deck to observe the sailing were immediately sent below to their quarters. A twin-engined PBY Catalina flying boat was scrambled and began circling the *Pasteur* overhead. Spotting the U-boat diving beneath the surface, the Catalina released two bombs, which found their target and exploded. A secondary explosion from under the surface was followed by an oil slick indicating that the U-boat had been destroyed. At that time, many of the young American GIs realised that they had experienced their first taste of action. The Catalina flying boat continued to circle overhead above the *Pasteur* like a guardian angel until fuel reserves depleted, forcing her to return to base. On her final pass the aircraft dipped for a low sweep over the *Pasteur*, dipping her wings to wave farewell. The *Pasteur* saluted in response, sounding three deafening blasts from her whistles.

An unsavoury record of this voyage worthy of mention was that 109 soldiers of the 5,000 on board were transferred to bunks in the former Bridal Suite. After settling down with their kit many rested in their bunks. After a short time many began to complain of itching on their legs and red blotches on their skin. After careful examination it was discovered that the mattresses on the bunk beds were alive and infested with ravenous jumping flees seeking replenishment after the previous hosts, the Italian POWs, had vacated. While the Bridal Suite was fumigated, the 109 US troops went down to the dining hall for much needed sustenance, but here the situation was further exacerbated, adding insult to injury, when what was presented on their plates was reheated leftovers from the Italian POWs! Needless to say, this led to loud vocal complaints and jeers.

Having safely reached the open sea, the *Pasteur* now headed due south towards Latin America. She remained vigilant, following a zigzag course to avoid submarine attack, changing course unpredictably every 2 to 10 minutes. Whilst at anchor at Freetown to take on supplies, a lookout spotted a periscope of a U-boat. Immediately, the ship was steamed and turned about before heading away at full speed following a zigzag course.

Stopping at Durban overnight on the 4–5 August, the troops on board were allowed very brief shore leave, but the *Pasteur* sailed early on 6 August. Ahead lay a terrible storm, where the ship is recorded as, 'dancing on a fiery sea'. Witness accounts from those on the bridge state that the ship was struck by a 'rogue monster killer wave' off the coast of South-east Africa. The course of the ship was easterly, heading directly into the storm when an enormous wave of 90–100ft (ten storeys high) swamped the *Pasteur*. It is said that the wave appeared out of the darkness and was an almost vertical wall of water, like a dark cliff face. The wave was preceded by a double-dip trough, which the crew referred to as a 'hole in the sea'. When the ship dipped down in the first trough, it then dipped alarmingly again into a second trough without rising on a wave. Immediately in front of the *Pasteur* the wall of water thunderously crashed down on to the bow, first with a white spray. Within a split second, the wall of water hit the bridge and engulfed the whole ship, causing it to be completely underwater! Someone on the bridge screamed, 'Is this it?' Another shouted in panic, 'We're going down!' Everyone prayed as the ship trembled and squealed like a pig as the immense water pressure outside pressed against the plates of the ship. On the other side of the glass windowpanes there was just solid water. What seemed like an eternity must have been just seconds, for suddenly the buoyancy of the air in the ship lifted her clear and she rose again to the surface, resurrected into the air. On the bridge, all power and instrumentation was temporarily lost. The captain suggested to those on the bridge that the giant rogue wave may have been caused by a combination of the strong current, the wind direction and some sort of underwater geological phenomenon. When power was restored after the storm had subsided, the captain addressed all those on board, announcing over the intercom, 'On any of the previous nine voyages, I have never encountered a worse storm.'

Much to the relief of all aboard, the *Pasteur* the ship docked in Suez on 16 August. On the following two voyages the ship carried 10,000 troops heading to join the British 8th Army, which was preparing for the Battle of El Alamein in North Africa. Each leg of the return voyages to the United States, calling at Durban, lasted 10 days.

On the first return voyage en route to Rio de Janeiro, Brazil, on 4 September 1942 the *Pasteur* encountered a silent ocean marauder prowling the South Atlantic. The German freighter, *Stier*, had been refitted with armaments by the Kriegsmarine and designated as a German auxiliary cruiser *Schiff 23*. This German raider was formally commissioned at the Wilton yards in Holland by Fregattenkapitan Horst Gerlach and named *Stier*, after his wife Hildegard's sign of the zodiac. *Stier* in German, means bull and represents the Taurus constellation.

Under the command of Fregattenkapitan Horst Gerlach the *Stier* secretly slipped out unnoticed into the Atlantic and was the last German raider to do so. The captain was satisfied with his young crew though they had not had much time to 'work up' and had been hampered by ice much of the time. Fregattenkapitan Gerlach found his ship generally to his liking in camouflage and armament (six 5.9in, two 37mm, four 20mm and two underwater torpedo tubes), but at 14½ knots she was slow. Hidden and waiting to pounce, north-west of the island of Tristan de Cunha, masked in the shadow of the remote volcanic archipelago, the forward lookouts on the *Stier* spotted through their Zeiss binoculars black smoke at a bearing of 33 degrees 30 minutes south and 15 degrees 45 minutes west. Someone shouted, 'Vessel in sight ahead. Alarm!' Germany's colours were hoisted as a visual signal to the obvious enemy ship, when the *Stier* was spotted. The identification of the unsuspecting approaching vessel was quickly established as the *Pasteur* because of her uniquely enormous funnel. In the German Kriegsmarine identification book, the silhouette of the *Pasteur* perfectly matched that of the approaching ship. Action stations was sounded on the *Stier* and the German raider quickly headed to intercept *Pasteur* at full speed with all guns and torpedo tubes manned.

Meanwhile, on the unsuspecting *Pasteur,* the forward port-side lookout spotted the German raider. Action stations was sounded on the troopship, which was carrying 1,000 German POWs guarded by 250 Polish soldiers. All boilers on the *Pasteur* were engaged and speed was rapidly increased to 27½ knots in an attempt to outrun the German foe. The chase was now on as *Pasteur* billowed out trailing clouds of inky black smoke. It was a race for survival. Would the *Pasteur's* boilers and engines withstand this demanding test? Somehow, inch by inch, over the next half an hour, *Pasteur* using her speed advantage placed a safe distance between her and the menacing German raider. Nevertheless, it was a very close near miss and the ship sailed at high alert in case her presence had been signalled ahead by the *Stier* to waiting wolf packs of German U-boats, until arriving at Rio on 8 September.

The *Pasteur* signalled details of the encounter to the Admiralty at Whitehall in London and the Royal Navy alerted all Allied shipping in the South Atlantic to be on the lookout for 'Raider J' (the British codeword for the German *Stier)*. After a cruise of 4½ months, in which she engaged and sank three ships, the German raider *Stier* was herself sunk on 27 September 1942, during a battle with an American cargo ship, the

SS *Stephen Hopkins,* which was also lost, just weeks after her encounter with the *Pasteur.*

The relief of a safe return for the *Pasteur* to Halifax was short-lived as on 29 September she set sail again for a transatlantic voyage, arriving at Greenock on 6 October.

1943

For much of the first part of 1943, the *Pasteur* is believed to have undergone an extensive refit at the Todds Dry dock in New York. The refit included: the fitting of additional anti-rolling keel plates under the hull, the construction of extra gun platforms for sixteen guns of two different calibres, the addition of ten further lifeboats (five stacked on each side), plus a new coat of grey camouflage paint.

The *Pasteur* was fuelled and made ready to sail from New York on 14 March on a transatlantic voyage to Liverpool, where she arrived on 23 March. After less than a week the *Pasteur* sailed again from Liverpool

This original and remarkable aerial reconnaissance photograph was taken on 26 November 1943 at 12.05 a.m. at an altitude of 400ft and shows the HMT *Pasteur* outbound from New York to Liverpool. (United States Navy/Britton Collection)

This original US Navy aerial photo was taken on 29 April 1943 and shows the troopship *Pasteur* at speed following a zigzag anti–submarine course. Note her bow is almost devoid of paint owing to several rough crossings of the Atlantic. (United States Navy/Ernest Arroyo Collection)

on 29 March with personnel of the Canadian Royal Air Force. En route, the new anti-roll keel plates were tested to the full when the ship was hit by a severe storm. The conclusion was that the new anti-roll plates were totally ineffective, providing little or no additional benefit. The *Pasteur* eventually arrived in Halifax on 5 April.

She returned to Liverpool on 9 April before crossing the Atlantic again for an intended arrival in New York on 28 April. Unfortunately, this planning schedule had to be revised as on 28 April the *Pasteur* broke down and stopped with engine problems on the Nantucket Bank approaching New York. Here, she remained stranded for two hours while urgent repairs were undertaken in some of the most dangerous U-boat-infested seas of the Atlantic. The US Navy immediately scrambled air support cover to circle the stricken vessel and the ship limped slowly into the Narrows entrance into New York Harbor Upper Bay on 29 April, anchoring off until Moran and US Navy tugs could assist. The *Pasteur* eventually docked on 30 April.

After patching up the mechanical problems, *Pasteur* was made ready to sail from New York on 5 May with troops from the 30th Signal Heavy Construction Battalion. As she sailed out of New York the gigantic troop ships, the former Cunard liners RMS *Queen Mary* and RMS *Queen Elizabeth* also sailed. Once clear of the Narrows beyond the Ambrose Lightship, the three troopships separated and each followed different courses. The *Pasteur* now steamed on a heading towards Casablanca, Morocco. The presence of German U-boats was detected and speed was increased, following a zigzag course. This action was successful and the ship made landfall at Casablanca on 12 May. Here the troops on board disembarked at 10.30 a.m. and were transported to the US base at Charles du Shane Camp.

The *Pasteur* returned to Halifax and at the end of May she received on board RAF pilots and ground crews following their training programmes. Two days into the voyage all those on board were awoken during the night by vibration in the ship. The usual cruising speed of the *Pasteur* was 24 knots, but on this occasion the speed was far in excess of this owing to the threat of submarine attack, causing considerable vibration.

The ship next embarked on contrasting voyages between the Arctic Circle and the tropics, but the problem of vibration whilst travelling at speed continued to plague those on board. At the end of May during a stay at Halifax, it was reluctantly agreed to remove decorative plaster décor and fittings in the restaurant in an attempt to cut down on vibration. The *Pasteur* once again sailed across the North Atlantic from Halifax, arriving in Liverpool on 30 June, before returning on 5 July. On arriving in Halifax, the fires were dropped and, after cooling, the boiler tubes and fireboxes were cleaned, with all leaking tubes replaced.

Aerial escort support cover was requested by the *Pasteur* when she sailed for the Clyde on 17 July, probably owing to the possible presence of German U-boats. She returned west across the Atlantic, arriving in New York on 9 August. The ship sailed east to Liverpool on 14 August and returned to the US again at reduced speed owing to a storm. A US Navy airship photographed *Pasteur* approaching North Carolina on 5 September. Upon arrival at the US Norfolk Naval Base, the *Pasteur* entered dry dock.

By mid 1943 the Allies had gained the upper hand in the Battle of the Atlantic. Air support was provided from Britain by Coastal Command Short Sunderland flying boat aircraft. On the other side of the Atlantic the threat posed by German U-boats was countered by US Navy twin-engined PBY Catalina flying boats. From May 1943 the mid-Atlantic gap (known as the 'Black Pit') was covered by US long-range four-engined B24 Liberator VLR aircraft. Escort carriers were also provided to support shipping and convoys crossing the Atlantic. These innovations provided greater safety for the *Pasteur,* but the threat of U-boat attack remained until the end of the war in Europe.

On 21 September, the *Pasteur* set out from Norfolk and arrived at its destination in Casablanca on 28 September. From here she sailed on to Dakar with 946 soldiers, arriving at Pier 8, Berths 45 and 46. Troops from the French colonies, 3,244 men of the 18th Senegalese Infantry Regiment, now boarded the *Pasteur*, plus members of the 1st and 2nd Batteries 105th Royal Artillery Regiment. Also joining the ship were survivors of the torpedoed French liner *De la Salle,* which had been sunk on 9 July 1943 by German U-boat U-508 captained by submarine ace Georg Staats.

The log record mentions that the *Pasteur* arrived at Casablanca with 4,500 troops before sailing on to reach New York on 29 October. The next day, 30 October, the entire ship was fumigated throughout followed by rat extermination! Records for 1943 reveal that on several voyages on the *Pasteur* complaints were received from American officers and GI troops regarding the quality of the food on board. Many complaints described it as 'terrible'.

From early November 1943 the *Pasteur* appears to have been based in and operated from New York for the intention of troop transport preparations for the D-Day invasion of Normandy on 6 June 1944. With this unstated aim in mind, the ship received three British female code decipherers on secret special duties, unaware of their long-term significance.

The voyage north from New York on 23 December to Halifax was void of any passengers, as all troops had disembarked at New York.

1944

The year 1944 was to begin with one of many transatlantic voyages conveying troops from North America to Britain in preparation for D-Day and the breakout from Normandy. The *Pasteur* arrived in Liverpool on 3 January from New York and briefly underwent a short refit before sailing again on 9 January. Repeat transatlantic voyages followed, but the voyage that commenced on 24 February took the ship to Plymouth in southern England. Upon arriving on 3 March, US forces bound for the first landings on Omaha Beach in June 1944 were disembarked. The ship was quickly turned around to head back over the Atlantic to New York, sailing again from New York on 13 March with members of the US Air Force and ground support crews from Seymour Johnson Field, whose immediate support was required in preparation for the build up to D-Day.

The next voyage sailed from New York on 29 May, arriving at Liverpool on 5 June. It brought members of the US Amphibious Brigade, the 973rd Engineer Maintenance Company, which was attached to the 9th Air Force and re-enforcement ground assault troops. It was noted that when a huge storm struck the ship whilst crossing the Atlantic the Amphibious Brigade did not feel the effects of seasickness but felt uncomfortable on seeing their land-based colleagues vomiting.

A new master, Captain R.G.B. Woollatt, took command of the *Pasteur* when sailing from Liverpool on 9 June. This distinguished Cunard captain was later to become the final master of the Cunard RMS *Aquitania,* taking her to the scrapyard in February 1950. On the return voyage from 20 June 1944 to 29 June 1944 between New York and Liverpool the ship conveyed 3,000 US troop reinforcements, sailing in an AT Convoy.

The logs indicate that during the summer of 1944 the *Pasteur* was briefly taken off the North Atlantic to transport troops to Durban, making stops at Freetown, Sierra Leone, on 7 July and Durban on 24 July. She returned to the North Atlantic in August to resume troop transport duties

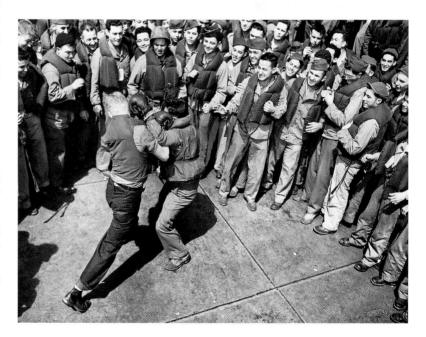

United States GIs bound for the European theatre of war via the port of Liverpool engage in a boxing match aboard the *Pasteur* in late April 1944. According to eyewitness accounts from members of the 101st Division, hundreds of dollars could change hands following the outcome of the bout and the boxing matches were serious encounters! (Associated Press/Britton Collection)

Above: The deck of the *Pasteur* is packed with American GIs to watch a dance and music concert in 1944. (Associated Press/Britton Collection)

Above right: Typical cramped sleeping arrangements aboard the HMT *Pasteur* These brave American GIs are bound for the beaches of Normandy and the D-Day invasion of Europe of 6 June 1944. (Associated Press/Britton Collection)

Right: A remarkable mid-Atlantic view. Passengers peer out from the depths of the *Pasteur* at the ships of a New York–Liverpool convoy in early May 1944. (Associated Press/Britton Collection)

between Halifax and Liverpool. Severe weather conditions delayed the sailing on 5 September, but she returned to New York in early November.

On 4 November, the *Pasteur* sailed alone from New York to Liverpool, conveying 10,000 GIs of the US 87th Infantry Division. Once out into the open sea, permission was granted to the commanding US Gunnery Officer from Captain Woollatt for troops to engage in practice firing the rear gun canon to aim at floating targets being towed from the ship. The US troops relaxing on the deck were ordered to move for their safety prior to firing commencing. Despite the strict orders from the firing team, the GIs did not move away. When the first shot was fired from the canon it ricocheted causing serious injury to four relaxing GIs. One casualty lost an eye and another lost part of his skull. All four GIs were rushed to the on-board field hospital to undergo emergency treatment.

Captain Woollatt returned across the Atlantic with the *Pasteur* to New York through a massive storm with 40ft waves in late November. On entering New York on 28 November, visible damage to the ship was observed, with buckled handrails along the decks, other fixtures and fittings, plus the absence of paintwork, caused by crashing waves. Remedial repairs were undertaken, but the missing paintwork was not restored on this visit.

The *Pasteur* sailed from New York on 30 November carrying 2,000 members of the US 788th Field Artillery Battalion and twelve 8in howitzers, plus members of the US Air Force. A Sunderland flying boat met the *Pasteur* off the north-west coast of Ireland on 7 December and two Royal Navy escort destroyers flanked her safely into the Port of Liverpool.

After returning to Liverpool on 9 December, a new master, Captain M. Bateman, took command of the *Pasteur* and remained in command for the next six months. His first voyage west was to convey war brides and their children to Halifax. The Canadian Royal Air Force signalled the *Pasteur* to alert them that German U-boats had been detected lurking around the approaches to Halifax and it was therefore decided to change course to New York. Returning to Halifax, the ship sailed again on 24 December to Liverpool. She sailed in very bad weather and was due to rendezvous with another fast 'Monster' liner, but the weather deteriorated to such an extent that radar contact was lost. The two super-fast liners were due to meet at 2.57 a.m., but contact was not established until 3.03 p.m. It is believed that the other vessel was the SS *Ile de France*. Travelling at an average of 24 knots, both ships arrived at Liverpool on 30 December.

1945

For the first few weeks of 1945 the *Pasteur* undertook regular voyages between New York, Liverpool and Quebec, all without any notable incidents or attack by German U-boats. On 14 February the *Pasteur* arrived at New York and after unloading she was towed to the Brooklyn Naval Yards to enter dry dock for intermediate refit.

After completion of the refit, the *Pasteur* was sent to Canada to transport 'Distressed British Seamen' (DBS) and return the British seamen home, many of whom had survived torpedo attack and survival at sea.

In the early hours of 1 May, all those on board the *Pasteur* learned that the German Führer, Adolf Hitler, had committed suicide the previous day and there now appeared to be some hope of an end to the war in Europe. A signal sent to the *Pasteur* on 5 May from the British Admiralty at Whitehall stated that the German Admiral Karl Dönitz had ordered that all U-boats cease operation. On 8 May there were great cheers and celebrations on board as the captain announced the news of the German surrender and cease fire.

With peace declared in Europe, the routine of transatlantic voyages was interrupted on 9 May when the ship was ordered to sail on a one-off return voyage to Port Said via the Straits of Gibraltar. The return voyage sailed from Port Said on 16 May and the ship was packed with celebrating British and Canadian troops, all making merry with the prospect of demob to return to their families.

On 31 May 1945 the *Pasteur* made her first visit to the Port of Southampton, which was to become her home port, instead of Liverpool. On 1 June, she sailed down the Solent to Portsmouth where she conveyed members of the Royal Canadian Air Force, Canadian troops and repatriated US GIs. Sailing alone, the *Pasteur* crossed the Atlantic, with all those on board excited and full of merriment.

Returning to Southampton on 13 June, a new ship's Master was appointed to take command of the *Pasteur*, Commodore Sir Cyril G. Illingworth, RD, RNR. This distinguished Cunard captain had immense experience at sea and had previously commanded the RMS *Queen Mary* and RMS *Queen Elizabeth* during the war. His delicate task was to oversee the transition of the management handover of the *Pasteur* to French authorities.

The *Pasteur* sailed from Southampton on 17 June, arriving at Halifax on 30 June. For some reason, the ship reduced speed en route in accordance with operational instructions, but resumed the normal pace of 22 knots on 28 June. On 4 July, the ship sailed once again from Halifax, heading towards her former home port at Liverpool, and at the last minute orders were radioed to the liner to change course for Southampton. On 16 July, the *Pasteur* sailed from Southampton to Quebec, but was diverted to call at London (the first and only time during her career as a troopship). Soon after setting out from the British capital on 18 July, revised orders were received to head to Halifax, which it reached on 22 July.

When the *Pasteur* returned to Southampton at the end of July, great changes presented themselves. On 1 August, the first contingent of French officers boarded the ship for familiarisation and integration.

Ongoing negotiations since the beginning of 1945 for the return of the *Pasteur* to the French flag and transfer of the management of the ship to the South Atlantique Line had ended with agreement that the ship would transfer to the French, but remain at the disposal of the Allies. A new French Master, Captain Lameignere, arrived via Dieppe, Newhaven and Waterloo to take command on 1 August.

The British crew were released from duties and the ship returned to total French control, ready and prepared to sail on 6 August. As soon as the last British members of the crew had departed from the ship, Captain Lameignere ordered a full inspection of the *Pasteur* with an inventory to be drawn up. After a briefing meeting on the foredeck whilst docked at Southampton, the French officers and crew inspected every item of machinery, boilers, bridge, oil tanks and pipework. It was during this inspection that a remarkable discovery was made. Upon lifting the cover of a water tank, still labelled in French, the inside of the tank was found to be packed full of the 'Pride of France': bottles of exquisite rare vintage wines and cognacs, all perfectly preserved. This hidden liquid windfall had remained hidden for over fives years, since the ship secretly sailed from Brest with the French gold reserves. The precious bottles of French wines had somehow not come to the attention of the British crews or any of the Allied troops, nor had their presence been discovered during any of the refits of the ship. All the bottles had escaped the war, survived battering from storms and travelled the world many times. Yet no one had examined the water tank! The question on the lips of the French captain and his crew was, 'Would the contents of the bottles still be palatable?' Captain Lameignere therefore ordered his curious crew to sample just a few bottles – for tasting purposes only! The *Pasteur* was closed and out of bounds to all visitors on the night of 4 August 1945 at 101 Berth, Southampton. British sailors and dock workers on the quayside looked on in curious amusement as the sound of French singing of 'La Marseillaise', laughter, merriment and celebration echoed along length of the New Docks: '*Vive la France.*'

In the late afternoon/early evening of 5 August, the recovering crew of the *Pasteur* embarked returning Allied troops bound for North America. She sailed on 6 August on the first of three round trips from Southampton to Quebec. Whilst at sea, several members of the Canadian Royal Air Force who were homebound fell ill with skin lesions and rashes. On examination, it was discovered that there was an outbreak of the highly contagious chickenpox on board the ship. On arriving in Quebec the epidemic on board was not declared to Canadian Immigration and Medical officers who boarded the *Pasteur*. Somehow, they did not meet the ship's doctor; otherwise the *Pasteur* would have been placed in quarantine. The undeclared presence of chickenpox resulted in great controversy and letters were exchanged between the Army HQ in Ottawa, the Canadian Immigration Department and the Veteran Affairs Department. As a consequence, it was agreed that all further inbound troopships, including the *Pasteur,* would be inspected by Medical Officer Chretien accompanied by Colonel Stone, a medic from the Canadian Royal Air Force.

On the second voyage between Southampton and Quebec, a complement of French officers and senior petty officers came on board the *Pasteur* to observe the operation of the ship and familiarise themselves with its workings. The official transfer of the flag of the *Pasteur* occurred at Southampton on 4 October, but the complete management and administration transfer to the French did not take place until 12 April 1946.

During the Second World War, the *Pasteur* had carried over 300,000 personal, including some 220,000 troops and 30,000 wounded. She had sailed 370,669 miles across the globe, but had proved expensive to operate. Her wartime British commanders expressed in official documentation their great concern that the ship had a propensity to make smoke, raising her visibility profile to U-boat and aerial attack. After the Second World War, the *Pasteur* repatriated US and Canadian troops from Europe to New York and Halifax. In October 1945, the *Pasteur* was formally returned to the French nation.

3

Compagnie de Navigation Sud Atlantique SS *Pasteur* 1946–57

(Tricolour French flag registered at Bordeaux)

Post War (April 1946–August 1957)

When the *Pasteur* was returned to the management of the Sud Atlantique in 1946, she remained in military service as a troopship and was used to transport French troops of the Leclerc Division to and from Indochina. The first return trip to her new base at Marseilles commenced on 27 January 1947, carrying 1,500 civilians and military evacuees, which included 350 sick and wounded soldiers. On 22 February, the *Pasteur* returned to Indochina, carrying 4,000 troop reinforcements. In October 1947, in recognition of her distinguished service, the *Pasteur* was presented with the nation's highest honour, the French Croix de Guerre.

The French Military Office of Maritime & Air Transport (BMTMA) took over the day-to-day operation of the ship to transport combatants. The maritime certificate for the *Pasteur* allowed 4,888 persons to be carried, which included the crew. However, in 1948, the BMTMA increased this to 5,000, but even this was exceeded on two voyages, with 5,173 and then 5,201 passengers and crew.

In theory, six decks were assigned to the French military and allocated according to rank. Enlisted men and non-commissioned officers were billeted on decks A, C, D, E and F, where they slept in huge blocks equipped with hammocks and mattresses. Some quarters, such as E9, could accommodate 250 men although it was very cramped; others, like A9, could only fit in 120 men. The non-commissioned officers did

not have it much better and the officers had to sleep in cabins varying in size from two to twenty-four, according to rank. Senior officers were two per cabin, captain and lieutenants nine to twelve per cabin. The officers slept in bunks, while the troops slept on mattresses or hammocks. Accommodation on board was strictly regulated, with officers and female staff benefiting from greater comfort, more space and a better food selection in the dining rooms. A policy of segregation was enforced on the ship, with different units being kept apart, and similarly with Europeans and North Africans.

As the *Pasteur* was generally overcrowded on these voyages, because of overcapacity, an officer travelling in the former Second-Class cabins would often be forced to eat in the former Third-Class facilities. In recognition of this, the French authorities compensated officers with a payment of 11,000 francs. This situation continued on board the ship until 1951. In the cabins accommodating twelve officers, there was only one sink and one shower, which meant queuing or setting up a rota for basic facilities. The situation was even worse for other ranks.

In 1950, the *Pasteur* made a 'one-off' voyage from Tandiong to Amsterdam to bring home Dutch people. She arrived in Amsterdam on 24 January 1950 with 4,000 soldiers and their families.

The permanent staff on the *Pasteur* during this period included: a commander of weapons who was usually a colonel, a deputy officer, four non-commissioned officers and five secretaries, plus a company of security personnel. The ship had two hospitals, one at the rear of the ship equipped with fifty beds on Deck C and three isolation booths for fourteen patients on Deck D. In September 1948, five doctors and fourteen nurses were provided. Four extra health workers were provided on the ship to assist with vaccines for malaria prophylaxis and checks for venereal diseases. On average, 1,300 consultations were provided per voyage. When the repatriations of injured soldiers commenced, an extra twenty nurses from the French Navy were sent to assist on the *Pasteur* and a further thirteen temporary recovery beds were installed at the aft end of the ship, just above the propellers!

When the eight on-board gendarmes assigned to security patrols were unavailable, members of the French Foreign Legion substituted to monitor decks, corridors, stairs and dormitories. With the excessive heat and humidity combined with cramped conditions providing little privacy it was not uncommon for heated disputes to break out onboard ship, which on occasions ended up with fighting, especially when gambling was involved. The on-board security patrols had to be especially vigilant when passing through the Suez Canal and the Strait of Malacca, as some troops decided that this could present an opportunity to jump overboard and desert. The *Pasteur* was equipped with a brig where those who fell foul of the law were locked up. The brig was also used for repatriating prisoners from Indochina to France, so the ship was in effect a floating barracks with all comprehensive military police services.

The logbooks of the ship record that in October 1948 there was serious fighting between members of the French paratroops, the 1st BEP and the 3rd BCCP. Similarly, in 1949 Algerian riflemen fought French Legionnaires during a voyage. Knife attacks during these outbreaks of violence were not uncommon. As a consequence of these violent outbreaks, it was decided to restrict all enlisted men to the lower decks. An exception was made for Muslims during the passage through the Red Sea, when they were allowed to pray on the upper decks in order for them to pray more easily towards Mecca.

Between 1946 and 1956, the *Pasteur* recorded eighty-one voyages. In 1948, extra precautions had to be taken when passing through the Suez Canal owing to the war between Israel and Egypt. Voyages normally commenced from an isolated dock at Estaque and La Joliette in Marseille. However, on several occasions, in order to avoid strikes and violent demonstrations, the BMTMA diverted the *Pasteur* to Cherbourg and Toulon. The stop at Cherbourg lengthened the voyage by 5 days, and troops had to leave the docks by train while gendarmes contained hostile anti-war protesting crowds.

A post–war French aerial photograph of the *Pasteur* underway in the Mediterranean Sea. (Britton Collection)

Life on board the *Pasteur* was punctuated by regular inspections, parades and evacuation exercises. Each morning and evening, as on all French warships, the Tricolour flag of France was raised and lowered with traditional honour. Routines were broken up by lectures on survival, disease and dangers of the country. Comfort distractions were introduced with the installation of seawater showers to limit the effects of heat and humidity. Bars were opened for officers in First Class and non-commissioned officers in Second Class, offering free chilled water. This water was discovered to be so stale that only bottled beer brought real refreshment. An onboard newspaper was introduced, updated by news received from radio broadcasts. Physical exercise sessions and volleyball games were organised on deck, and a Sunday Mass. Twice per week, adventure films were shown to entertain the French troops on board. Perhaps the most popular activities on the troopship at this time were the boxing matches and theatrical evenings. Many, however, preferred to pass the time with endless card games.

The food on board the *Pasteur* was at times lacking in traditional high standards of French cuisine. Several voyages record collective food poisoning. In June 1948, there is a record of two waves of gastrointestinal syndromes which triggered an investigation into the possibility of poisoning or attempted sabotage of the food supply. The assessment of the Maritime Registration Inspectorate was that there was nothing detectable and suspicion fell on the food hygiene and preparation. On occasions, there are recorded instances of French patriots donating fruit, beer and cigarettes to be distributed to all the French troops on board when the ship stopped at Port Said or Aden.

This photograph of the *Pasteur* is believed to have been taken at Suez in 1956. (William Paulus Collection)

Normally, the return voyages of the *Pasteur* from Marseille in southern France to Indochina lasted about 5 weeks, 15–16 days for the outward voyage, 2–7 days for landing and boarding men, mail, and materials, and 16–17 days for the return voyage. After returning to Marseille, the routine was over the next 10–15 days to disinfect and fumigate the ship, make repairs, refuel and replenish before the ship could sail again. Voyages from Marseille to Indochina would sail via Port Said, Aden and Singapore for refuelling and water stops. There were variations depending on circumstances with stops at Algiers, Mers-el-Kebir and Bizerte. Upon arriving in Indochina, the *Pasteur* would usually disembark passengers via landing craft and anchor off Cape St Jacques as her draft would not allow the ship to venture up the Saigon river. At all ports where the ship called, a security exclusion perimeter of 1,000m was established to prevent local water-bound hawkers from coming alongside the ship. Armed French marines in fast patrol boats would circle the *Pasteur* and rigorously enforce this ruling. From Cape St Jacques, the ship would usually sail north to anchor off Turan before arriving at Halong Bay in North Vietnam.

An examination of the French logbooks of the *Pasteur* reveals a numerical imbalance between many outward and return voyages. On the voyage commenced on 4 April 1948, the ship transported 4,056 men on the outward voyage, but returned with only 1,336 men, of which 287 were wounded or sick troops. The arrival of the *Pasteur* at Marseille often triggered intense agitation by opponents of the Indochina War of the French CGT and the PCF protest movements. To begin with, boarding and disembarking of the ship with troops was serenaded with musical bands, but as opinions changed, this all changed. French protestors shouting insults began pelting the *Pasteur* with rotten tomatoes and eggs, which in time escalated to metal bolts. Even the wounded troops on stretchers coming off the ship were booed, heckled and spat at, such was the anti-war feeling at the quayside. Arrivals and departures of the *Pasteur* were therefore made under cover of darkness and under police protection.

Management of the *Pasteur* was transferred to the Chargeus Reunis Company in 1952.

Between 1947 and 1953, the *Pasteur* transported over 500,000 troops and passengers between France, North Africa and Indochina, a staggering 24.2 per cent of the overall total in the campaign, making thirty-nine round trips. At some time, nearly half of the French combatants travelled aboard the ship. Thus the *Pasteur* acquired a certain mystique in France as stories about the ship were related to friends and relatives of the veterans of the war. At the end of the Indochina War, the *Pasteur* remained at the

A British squaddie with his rifle watches the *Pasteur* steam through the Suez Canal in 1956. (Associated Press/Britton Collection)

disposal of the French Forces. The ship found some short-haul work in the Mediterranean, with voyages to Algeria.

Between July and late August 1956 the *Pasteur* was laid up at Toulon, but she was reactivated in September and prepared for immediate re-entry to service. The *Pasteur*, along with other civilian and military ships, was designated to transport troops during the Suez Canal Crisis. The General Headquarters for French troops was on board the *Pasteur* and she was moored in Port Said Harbour until 22 December 1956. The ship was one of the last Allied vessels to sail from Port Said at the end of the Suez Crisis, evacuating 2,822 French troops – two regiments of parachutists and a large contingent of soldiers. On 24 December, Christmas Mass was held in the vast dining saloon and on 26 December the ship arrived in Algeria.

For the second time in her career, the *Pasteur* was decorated with the award of the Croix de Guerre in recognition of services to the French nation. She had now travelled an incredible 1.5 million miles and had carried 850,000 troops during her career.

On 26 January 1957 the *Pasteur* sailed again to lay up at Brest on 31 January 1957 and remained inactive for seven months, with only a skeleton crew on board the ship.

With trooping duties concluded, rumours circulated that the grand heroic lady, the *Pasteur*, would be refitted to luxury standards. Some consideration was certainly given to restoring the *Pasteur* to her former glory and transferring her to the French Line as a temporary replacement for the ageing *Ile de France*. However, the new 66,000-ton prestige project for the construction of the new superliner, SS *France*, was already confirmed and it was intended that this new flagship liner would replace both the *Ile de France* and her running mate *Liberté*. After much discussion it was decided to offer *Pasteur* for sale.

4

North German Lloyd TS Bremen
1957–72

(West German flag registered at Bremen)
32,336 gross tonnage 1957–66
32,360 gross tonnage 1966–72

In 1955, Allied restrictions on the German ownership of passenger ships were lifted. The North German Lloyd was eager to restore something of its pre-War Bremerhaven–New York transatlantic service. The 19,100 ton *Berlin*, the former Swedish American *Gripsholm* built in 1925, was quickly acquired. However, North German Lloyd, under the direction of the dynamic Richard Bertram, was seeking a larger, faster and more luxurious ocean liner.

On learning that the *Pasteur* was for sale at Brest, North German Lloyd decided to place a serious offer on the table for the purchase of the ship. After fruitful negotiations in early August, the sale of the ship was agreed for £2 million or approximately DM20 million and contracts signed and exchanged, dated 18 September 1957. The news of the sale causes consternation everywhere. In Paris there wass outrage that the pride of France has been sold to Germany. In the French National Assembly there was official opposition to the sale of the beloved *Pasteur* to a foreign and ex-enemy power. Senator Michel Debra demanded that the Advisory Council release full details of the sale. The Secretary of State for the French Marine stated that the money received from the sale would go directly towards to financing of the construction of the SS *France*. Outside the French Assembly, the sale of *Pasteur* sparked violent protests and confrontation with the French Gendarmerie. In the shipping offices in London and Lisbon, the question heard was, 'Have these North German Lloyd people lost their mind [*sic*]?'

In early September, all remaining French wine reserves in store on board the *Pasteur* were transferred ashore along with expensive items of silver cutlery and plates.

The ship, towed by two NDL tugs, was transferred to Bremerhaven on 26 September, with thirty-one technicians and 100 crew members aboard. The top section of her gigantic funnel was removed and she arrived at Vegesack some days later. A three-month period of time was spent at the here. Troopship facilities were completely removed to leave the vessel almost an empty shell. On 8 January 1958, the former *Pasteur* was towed from Bremerhaven to Bremen, where reconstruction of the ship commenced on 10 January. Structurally, the most noticeable change was a new 52½ft-high funnel. The new funnel had the advantage of being more sophisticated with a streamlined technological profile. In addition to the new funnel, a new radar mast was installed above the bridge, replacing her tall pole masts. The new ship entered dry dock at Bremerhaven for remaining fitting out, painting of the hull, overhaul of the screws and the installation of four new La Mont-type boilers, generators and Denny-Brown stabilisers fitted amidships.

Eight of the original ten boilers were removed, but two were retained as auxiliaries. The four HP and MP turbines were replaced by ones from Compagnie Electro Mécanique, which had originally provided *Pasteur*'s machinery. The engine plant was extensively modernised to handle the greater electrical output the new *Bremen* would require. After 500 days in the Bremer Vulkan shipyard the new TS *Bremen* left to return to Bremerhaven.

Following the sale of the ship to North German Lloyd, the ship is pictured undergoing conversion and refit to become the TS *Bremen*. This picture records the very moment the new funnel was lowered into place by the gigantic floating crane at the Bremer Vulkan shipyard. (Associated Press/Britton Collection)

Luxury accommodation was built for 216 first-class and 906 tourist-class passengers. Air conditioning was provided throughout. New interiors were ultra-modern and employed some of the latest materials. Plexiglas, aluminium and fireproof textiles abounded and, although following the modifications to the ship no two-deck-high spaces remained, the new *Bremen* was a roomy and fascinating ship. The only spaces on the ship that remained unaltered were the wide promenade deck, the bridge and part of the culinary department, albeit with completely new, modern equipment.

Visually the ship had a more modern appearance, as the original masts were removed and more modern short streamlined ones provided on the superstructure. The gigantic old funnel was removed, and a new straw-coloured funnel replaced it. Gravity davits were fitted for boats on the upper deck, and the decks were altered. Her gross tonnage was now 32,336 tons with a speed of 23 knots. The complete refit had cost in excess of £6.5 million or approximately DM65 million.

A fascinating shot of the TS *Bremen* in dry dock at Bremerhaven, revealing her hull and propeller blades. The size and scale of the ship can be appreciated by the size of the dock worker standing beneath the ship. (Associated Press)

Onlookers cheer and wave as the TS *Bremen* is moved by tugs ready for her departure on her maiden voyage. (Associated Press/Britton Collection)

The TS *Bremen* at New York on her maiden voyage on 16 July 1959. She is receiving the traditional New York welcome from local fireboats with a plume of spray. (Associated Press/Britton Collection)

This aerial publicity photograph was arranged by North German Lloyd in 1961. It shows the inbound German flagship TS *Bremen* making her way up the Hudson River in New York past her outbound smaller running mate, the MS *Berlin*. The liner's paths crossed in New York Harbor only once before, in July 1959 when the *Bremen* arrived following her maiden voyage. (Associated Press/Britton Collection)

Tragedy struck during the fitting out at Bremer Vulkan at 8.10 p.m. on 30 April. A high-pressure steam leak between the boiler room and the funnel was caused when a valve from the main line broke, emitting 400 degrees heat. Four workers were killed and a fifth was admitted Blumenthal Hospital with life-threatening injuries. Two other workers who were working just below the funnel miraculously escaped with minor injuries.

The logbook for Wednesday 1 July reveals that the new TS *Bremen* began to receive fresh supplies for the food stores, refrigerators and the new locked liquor storage facility of the finest quality German wines from the Mosel region, including: Riesling, Rheingau, Spätburgunder and Bernkasteler. These fine wines were accompanied by crates of the best German beers: Holsten Pilsener, Jever, Diebels Alt, Franziskaner Weissbier and Oettinger. Top of the list of foods being loaded aboard the new German flagship were several tons of traditional German *Wurst* (sausages), *Sauerbraten* (pickled roast) and *Schnitzel* (thin boneless cutlets of meat).

On Friday 3 July at 12.35, the gleaming new ship was christened with the name *Bremen* – the fifth ship to bear this name. The contemporary-looking two-class ocean liner became West Germany's new flagship and formally entered service with a 7-hour shakedown cruise.

Proud cheering crowds thronged every vantage point on 9 July as the new TS *Bremen* sailed from Bremerhaven on her maiden voyage with her Master, Captain Heinrich Lorenz, at the helm, to New York from Bremerhaven to Cherbourg and Southampton. The triumphant entry into New York on 16 July was met with the customary welcome of plumes of spray from fireboats reserved for first-time transatlantic passenger liners. She berthed once again at French Line's Pier 88, West 48th Street. By coincidence, in the opposite berth was French Line's *Liberté*. A local newspaper reporter found it entertaining material and in the next edition of the *New York Times* he wrote an amusing story featuring the two ocean liners – one liner was former French and now German, while the other was ex-German and now French. The *Liberté* had been the record-breaking *Europa* of 1930 and the new TS *Bremen* was of French pedigree.

Following the glitz of an afternoon press conference held on board the new *Bremen*, seamen from both the *Liberté* and the *Bremen* gazed curiously across the pier at each others' ocean liners. Timidly at first, they began to cross over, and by late afternoon 100 French sailors had ventured aboard the *Bremen* and a similar number of Germans had walked up the gangway to inspect the elegant French *Liberté*. Over the next few years, the crew of the *Bremen* were to become a very popular and highly thought-of group of seamen. They actively participated in the North Atlantic Football Trophy, which was a football competition held between representative teams of the ocean liners of the North Atlantic. The British Cunard crews regarded the *Bremen* team as very skilful, well organised and determined with fast wingers. The *Bremen* team was very successful and built an enviable international reputation.

Over the next few months, the *Bremen* established herself as a fine luxury liner of the North Atlantic. On 7 December during a winter voyage, soon after sailing from Cherbourg, she encountered a hurricane with 120mph winds and 40ft waves. The ship's logbook records that the barometer dramatically fell from 1,000 to 965 millibars. A weather report from the First Radio Officer confirmed a storm warning with the centre of the weather activity located at 47.5 degrees north, 1.5 degrees west. Within minutes, the wind speed increased to storm force 9, forcing the ship to reduce speed from 20 to 18 knots. By the afternoon, the weather conditions had deteriorated further to become a full hurricane with wind speed increasing to 130mph. This caused the *Bremen* to reduce her speed to a mere 9 knots for the next 24 hours. The strength of the crashing waves smashed five portholes and the glass on three promenade deck windows.

Captain Günter Rössing, master of the TS *Bremen*, took command of the North German Lloyd flag ship in 1960. He was always very proud of his ship, TS *Bremen*, and he offered a warm welcome to visitors when calling at different ports around the world. (Associated Press/Britton Collection)

The new stabilisers were successfully deployed and transformed performance to demonstrate that the ship had overcome the previous problems of pitching and rolling in her former life as the *Pasteur*. The only significant damage was to some panes of glass and the 8cwt bronze ship's bell. As the huge waves crashed over the decks of the *Bremen*, the ship's bell was torn from its anchorage on the forecastle and tossed helplessly into a shaft groove. Captain Lawrence, who was on the bridge for 2½ days continuously, dismissed with a gesture that he was imprisoned for all this time. He said, 'My ship has proven itself in every way. The stabilisers have prevented passenger seasickness and proved the ship is very efficient.' Remarkably, the *Bremen* was able to make up time and arrived in New York at 8 a.m. on 13 December, just 10 minutes late!

On a subsequent voyage, Captain Günter Rössing of the *Bremen* heroically responded to a distress call from the US freighter *Wolverine*. What followed was a dramatic rescue one Sunday morning off Cherbourg in high seas. A lifeboat was launched from the *Bremen* to come to the assistance of a 9-year-old child with acute appendicitis. The sick child, called Ruykert Fowler, was transferred aboard the lifeboat wrapped in blankets firmly on a stretcher. The return of the lifeboat to the *Bremen* was severely hampered by stormy waves, with troughs of 15ft. The whole rescue manoeuvre lasted from 11 a.m. until 3 p.m.. The boy's father, who was director of the US Bethlehem Steel Company, accompanied his son on board the *Bremen*. He was very relieved to step aboard the *Bremen* and thanked Captain Rössing and all the crew of the ship for saving his son's life. He said, 'I thought the rescue manoeuvre would never end, but I had total confidence that it would succeed.' On board the *Bremen*, the ship's doctor made ready the operating theatre in the hospital. The successful operation on the child took 1½ hours. The *Bremen*'s captain added that he had only been involved in three ship-to-ship rescues during his 42–year career at sea, but this one had provided him with the most worry.

The crew of the *Bremen* always respected and admired wildlife, often throwing gulls leftovers to eat. They also recalled enjoying watching flying fish in the tropical waters when cruising, but sadly on one voyage across the Atlantic, the *Bremen* unavoidably collided with a whale which wrapped itself around the bow of the ship.

North German Lloyd sent the *Bremen* cruising during the off–peak season and this commenced in the winter of 1960. Cruises were generally from New York to the Caribbean, but on occasions there were also cruises to the Baltic Sea. On one such cruise, the ship called at Stockholm. Bright sunshine and music from the harbour attracted hundreds of onlookers to watch from the quay. They waved enthusiastically as the flagship of the North German Line gently sailed from the Swedish port. Two Swedish pilots were present on the bridge of the *Bremen* to guide safely her through the busy waters of Stockholm Harbour. A fleet of sailing yachts, sightseeing motor boats and local ferries followed the *Bremen*. Suddenly, on the bridge of the *Bremen* the alarm sounded. Immediately ahead of the *Bremen* a helpless motor boat with a broken engine was on a collision course with the ship. The captain sounded the ship's booming whistle and placed the 32,000-ton vessel into reverse. Unfortunately, it was too late and the bow of the *Bremen* sliced through the flimsy wooden motorboat and the sicken sound of splintering wood could be clearly heard by those lining the decks of the ship. Above on the deck of the *Bremen*, passengers and crew watched helplessly as two people were fighting in the bow waves of the liner for their lives. Sadly, it was all too late.

Bad luck followed the TS *Bremen* on the Baltic Sea cruise from Bremerhaven on 30 June 1964. The ship unfortunately rammed the quay at the northern Polish port of Gdynia Gdansk. According to Captain Rössing, this occurred because the whistle of the Polish pilots on board the *Bremen* was not heard by the tugboats. The German liner had to repeat the signal to the tugs three times and the collision with the quay damaged some wooden support beams.

Whilst under the direction of two Swedish pilots, the bad luck on this voyage continued, as on the return to Stockholm the *Bremen* ran aground entering Stockholm as it passed through the narrow archipelago. In the port of Stockholm, the *Bremen* lost an anchor. Those on the bridge of the *Bremen* recall that Captain Rössing shook his head in despair, looked to the Heavens and muttered the word, *'Scheiße!'*

During the winter of 1962–63, a severe cold snap hit Western Europe. In Bremerhaven, the TS *Bremen* encountered frozen seas, blizzards and small ice flows, which hampered sailings. A voyage across the Solent past Ryde, Isle of Wight and up Southampton Water also encountered sea ice, previously unheard of in British waters. On docking at Southampton, there was a deep covering of snow along the quayside at 107 Berth and the freezing arctic conditions were such that it was almost impossible to secure a line as the ropes on the ship were frozen solid and not flexible. The gangways had to be salted and gritted for safety as passengers disembarking and embarking, frequently slipped on black ice. Dockside cranes failed as they too were frozen, and it was unavoidably decided to abandon the movement of heavy loads from ship to shore and vice versa. Instead, the heavy items remained secured in the hold of the ship for a

The passing of namesakes, the North German Lloyd TS *Bremen* and a scale model of her predecessor carrying the name *Bremen*. (Associated Press/Britton Collection)

Twilight arrival of the TS *Bremen* at her home port of Bremerhaven. (Associated Press/ Britton Collection)

A close–up view of the scale model of the original *Bremen*. (Associated Press/ Britton Collection)

round trip across the Atlantic to New York and were unloaded when the *Bremen* docked at Southampton next time!

At the end of January in 1964, transatlantic services operating into New York were interrupted by a tugboat strike. For several weeks the whole of the Port of New York was paralysed by the strike of 3,500 tug men. This caused massive disruption to services which were cancelled or transferred to other ports. Some ocean liners attempted to successfully dock and sail without the aid of tugs. The *Bremen* was one such liner which cautiously sailed up the fast-flowing River Hudson with its challenging tides. Whilst docking, there was the risk of strong gusts of wind which could have a tremendous affect due to the sheer size of the liner. By using the arm of the pier as a pivot and gauging the flow of the tide down the Hudson, Captain Rössing used all his immense knowledge of seamanship, skills and experience to dock the *Bremen*. On 4 March, at the exact point

Looking out from the shadows of the Columbus Quay Passenger Terminal at Bremerhaven, spectators watch the departure of the TS *Bremen*. (Britton Collection)

A spectacular aerial view at from above the Columbus Quay at Bremerhaven showing the arrival of the TS *Bremen* as she is gently hauled into position on the quayside, just ahead of her running mate the MS *Berlin*. (Richard Weiss Collection)

of high tide on the Hudson River, Captain Rössing slipped the *Bremen* from her berth earlier than scheduled. Crowds lined the shore, many of whom were the striking tug men who could quickly identify any signs of trouble. Everyone waited nervously, many with cameras at the ready, but the *Bremen*'s manoeuvre backing out into the Hudson River was a lesson in perfection. As the ship prepared to turn down stream towards the Narrows, an urgent message was received on the bridge that, because of the early sailing, some of the passengers had missed the boat. A motorised lifeboat was therefore quickly lowered and dispatched to collect the stranded passengers and their luggage. Shortly afterwards, members of the Tugboat Crewmen's Union voted to end their 33-day-old strike.

Captain Günter Rössing was always very proud of the *Bremen* and he offered a warm welcome to visitors when calling at different ports around the world. His smile and firm handshake made one feel immediately at ease. Quite often accompanying him on board when calling into Southampton was his faithful friend, a small dog. Sadly, this great sea captain and Master of the *Bremen* passed away at sea on the bridge at

the halfway mark on a voyage between Bremerhaven and New York on Tuesday 3 August 1965 at the age of just 63 years. Captain Rössing was a veteran of more than 40 years with the North German Line. The *Bremen*'s chief executive officer took command of the ship, but the shocking news of Captain Rössing's sudden death was greeted with great sadness by all his many friends on board, both passengers and crew.

At the end of 1965, North Germen Lloyd purchased the former Swedish American Line *MS Kungsholm* and renamed her *Europa*. She joined the *Bremen* on North Atlantic services and cruising. Meanwhile, the *Berlin* was paid off as surplus to requirements. Lavish marketing brochures and posters were produced for the 1966 season showing off the new *Europa* and *Bremen*.

During the winter of 1965–66 refit, the *Bremen* had a large bulbous bow fitted just below the waterline. The bulb modified the way the water flowed around the hull, reducing drag and thus increasing speed, range, stability and fuel efficiency by at least 12 per cent. The introduction of the bulbous bow on the *Bremen* also increased the buoyancy of the forward

The race is on! Over–enthusiastic schoolboys in their sailing dinghy try their hand at racing alongside the TS *Bremen*. (William Paulus)

Dressed overall, the TS *Bremen* sails majestically down the Hudson in New York. Note the open shell door with the crew awaiting the pending transfer of the harbour pilot. (William Paulus)

At the end of January in 1964, transatlantic services operating into New York were interrupted by a tugboat strike. For several weeks, the whole of the Port of New York was paralysed by the strike of 3,500 tug men. This caused massive disruption to services which were cancelled or transferred to other ports. Some ocean liners attempted to successfully dock and sail without the aid of tugs. On 4 March at the exact point of high tide on the Hudson River, Captain Rössing slipped the Bremen from her berth earlier than scheduled. Crowds lined the shore, many of whom were the striking tug men who could quickly identify any signs of trouble. Everyone waited nervously many with cameras at the ready, but the *Bremen*'s manoeuvre backing out into the Hudson River was a lesson in perfection. As the ship prepared to turn down stream towards the Narrows, an urgent message was received on the bridge that because of the early sailing some of the passengers had missed the boat. A motorised lifeboat was therefore quickly lowered and dispatched to collect the stranded passengers and their luggage. Shortly after members of the Tugboat Crewmen's Union voted to end their 33–day–old strike. (Associated Press/Britton Collection)

part and hence reduced the pitching of the ship, which had previously plagued her since being built as the *Pasteur*. Her gross tonnage was increased to 32,320 tons.

Further improvements to the German flagship were made during the winter of 1970–71 refit (November 1970 to January 1971) including: a new boutique, a new photo shop, an outdoor pool, new carpeting throughout extending to corridors, lobbies, stairs, staterooms, lounges and dining rooms. Four new boats for tendering were delivered and fitted to the ship. This expensive investment was directed at the cruise market and was viewed by many as securing the future of the TS *Bremen*. Yet, within a mere 9 months the flag ship of Hapag Lloyd would be sold.

Between March 1967 and the summer of 1971, the *Bremen* began to experience engine and boiler problems, forcing her to delay and even cancel planned voyages. In the boiler room, cracked and leaking boiler stays were discovered. On another occasion, a boiler failed, requiring a new replacement tube plate. Crew members recall that the *Bremen*'s boilers also failed with blown super-heater heads on one voyage, causing the ship to stop temporarily in mid-Atlantic. Sometimes an ageing boiler tube would blow, although this could be temporarily caulked, but the issues of reliability of the *Bremen* were an great ongoing concern to the management and were causing financial loss through loss of income and a requirement for repair and investment.

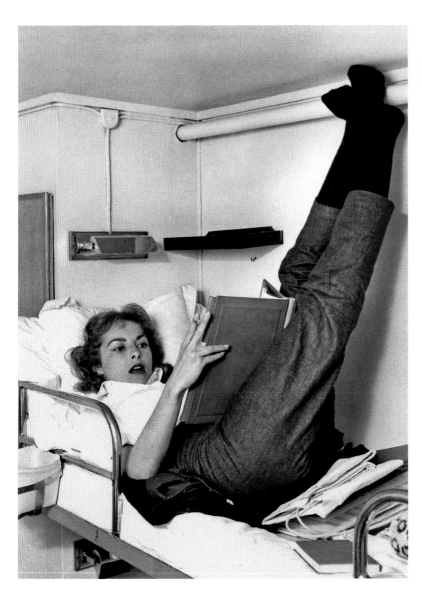

Hollywood screen siren, Janet Leigh, is captured reading her lines for her next film in a bunk on the TS *Bremen* bound for New York. (Associated Press/Britton Collection)

It always exciting to wander along Luxury Liner Row at New York and watch the parade of ocean liners. This was the view on 31 May 1962 with the Cunard RMS *Queen Mary* seen sailing from Pier 90 to Cherbourg and Southampton. Also pictured are, from bottom to top: American Export Line SS *Constitution*, United States Line SS *America* and SS *United States*, North German Lloyd TS *Bremen*, Cunard *Sylvania* and Moore McCormack *Brasil*. (Associated Press)

From the early 1960s, the effects of competition from transatlantic air travel began to take their toll on passenger receipts of the TS *Bremen*. With the introduction of the American Boeing 707 and British Comet aircraft, journey times across the Atlantic were cut dramatically and, linked to attractive cheaper air fares, passenger numbers on the *Bremen* plummeted. Accumulated repairs to the boilers and turbines on the *Bremen* caused the owners, Hapag Lloyd (after the merger of North German Lloyd with the Hamburg American Line in September 1970), to consider the future of the ship. Supplementary income from cruising in the winter months with the *Bremen* was just not enough to subsidise non-profitable North Atlantic voyages, especially as fuel costs were beginning to escalate.

After 175 Atlantic crossings and 117 cruises, Hapag Lloyd reluctantly agreed to sell the TS *Bremen* on 28 October 1971 for DM40 million to International Cruises, a division of Chandris Cruises of Greece. The *Bremen* arrived for the last time, after crossing the Atlantic, in her home port of Bremerhaven on 22 December 1971. She made a farewell New Year cruise and returned to the Bremerhaven Columbus Quay for the final time on 12 January 1972 at 8 a.m. Throughout the next three days from the morning of 12 January all precious liquor stores of German wines and beers were brought ashore from the ship, plus cutlery, plates, bed linen and precious items to be retained. Many serving and former members of the crew took this opportunity to visit aboard their *Bremen* to pay their last respects, some of whom were able to liberate souvenirs from the ship to cherish and treasure as a lasting memory.

During her North German Lloyd/Hapag Lloyd career the TS *Bremen* had sailed 1,618,547 nautical miles and consumed 954,857 tons of fuel oil whilst underway at sea. The total consumption of fuel including times in port and during refits amounted to 1,029,000 tons.

The price of fame! When film star Curd Jürgens sat down for his dinner in the first-class lounge on TS *Bremen* he was quickly spotted by fellow passengers eager for his autograph – much to the displeasure of those diners sitting alongside him. (Britton Collection)

Greeting the not-so-famous at the gala dinner aboard the TS *Bremen*. A handshake and welcome from the captain of the TS *Bremen* to a gala dinner was always a memory to be treasured. (Britton Collection)

North German Lloyd TS *Bremen:* Key Facts

Weight: 32,336 tons

Dimensions: 697ft x 88ft

Number of decks: 12 (four of which were continuous)

Draught: 30ft 7in

Passengers: 216 First Class, 906 Tourist Class

Crew Total: 544 (100 on deck, 76 mechanical staff, 70 kitchen staff, 232 staff engaged as pursers, secretaries, administrators, nurses, nursery, beauticians, hairdressers, tailors, musicians, etc).

Kitchen Staff: 1 premier first class chef, 4 butchers, 1 leading chef tourist class, 6 bakers, 2 chef 'wizards', 3 pantry men, 7 *Koche*, 3 pantry assistants, 8 second cooks, 2 coffee cooks, 7 third cooks, 1 *Oberkochmaat*, 2 team cooks, 19 *Kochmaaten* and 4 confectioners.

Famous sisters aboard the TS *Bremen*. (Britton Collection)

The Captains of *Bremen*

Heinrich Lorenz (1959–60)
Fritz Leusner (1960)
Günter Rössing (1960–65)
Behnsen (1965–69)
Walter Bulkhead (captain agencies around 1969)
Paul Vetter (1969–71)
Claus Hamje (1971–72)

Official Numbers and Code Letters

Official numbers were a forerunner to IMO Numbers. The *Pasteur* had the UK official number 166305 and used the code letters FNDC until 1940 and GNDW from 1940 to 1946.

5

Chandris Cruises Regina Magna
1972–77

(Greek flag registered at Piraeus)
23,801 gross tonnage 1972–77

The ship now entered dry dock in preparation for her transfer to the new owners. The hull was cleared of barnacles, a boiler survey and light intermediate overhaul were undertaken and the new name, *Regina Magna*, was stencilled onto her bows, and the embossed lettering *Bremen* was painted over and Greek lettering painted on her bow on 17 January 1972. An official handover ceremony was held on 19 January when the flags were lowered and presented by TS *Bremen*'s Captain Paul Vetter to the new owner Demitri Chandris. It was the end of an era and many of the *Bremen*'s former crew watched silently and tearfully as their flagship passed into Greek hands. Still in her North German Lloyd livery, on 21 January the new *Regina Magna* sailed from Bremerhaven to commence her new career as a Mediterranean cruise ship.

On arrival in Greece, the painters set to work and the *Regina Magna* was transformed, with her funnel painted in dark blue with a narrow black top and large white 'X', an all white hull with red boot topping, but otherwise little altered externally. Internally, Greek-lettered labels and signs began to appear with a few Chandris Cruise promotional displays, but the ship remained largely as before. What had changed was the cuisine of the ship

Chandris Line TS *Regina Magna* at Tilbury Docks on 31 August 1973. (Clive Harvey)

to a more buffet style. On the menu now were traditional Mediterranean Greek dishes: moussaka (oven-baked casserole filled with spicy meat), tiropites (triangular pastries filled with a mixture of Greek cheeses), baklava (cinnamon and nut-filled pastries) and horta vrasta (boiled leafy greens). In the lounge passengers were served with traditional Greek ouzo alcoholic liquor, which the author found delightful to sample. This was followed by Agiorghitiko red wine or chilled Moschofilero white wine, depending on the dish to be eaten.

Regina Magna inaugurated her Mediterranean service, calling at Limassol for the first time on 19 May, taking passengers from Cyprus to Beirut, Haifa, Heraklion, Piraeus, Katakolon, Corfu, Dubrovnik and Venice. On 25 May 1972 the new *Regina Magna* docked at Tilbury Docks, London, for the first time. She sailed two days later on 27 May on a mini-cruise. The ship was now returned to more familiar waters to sail from Southampton on 9 June under the banner of the Chandris Blue Cruises. Returning to the Mediterranean, she continued to call at Limassol every fortnight and her cruises became very popular. More adventurous cruises were introduced, sailing from Amsterdam, London and Southampton to Scandinavia and the Baltic ports, and from Genoa to West Africa. However, the management of Chandris assessed these longer cruises to be uneconomic, offering little financial return owing to the great deal of fuel required.

Within two years, the ship was taken out of service on 17 October 1974. The new Greek owners considered her to be too dear to operate owing to rising fuel costs and the consumption of oil by an ageing vessel. The 1974, fleet list for the newly merged Chandris Cruises and Chandris Line did not include the *Regina Magna*, which was laid up and placed into a state of idleness with a skeleton crew at the port of Piraeus. Her future was uncertain and her paintwork began to deteriorate rapidly under the blistering sun. Here, the mothballed ship remained silently at anchor for almost three years awaiting her fate. Would she be offered for scrapping?

Philippine Singapore Ports Corporation
Saudi Phil 1 1977–80

(Saudi Arabian flag registered at Jeddah)

An offer to purchase the redundant vessel was received from the Philippine Singapore Ports Corporation and following successful negotiations agreement was made for the purchase of the ship pending transfer to Jeddah, Saudi Arabia as an accommodation ship for 3,500 Filipino workers. On 6 October 1977, the ship was renamed *Saudi Phil 1* and was slowly and ignominiously towed by tugs, arriving in Jeddah on 1 November 1977.

Externally, her funnel was painted green with a new insignia on a white background, but the livery of her hull and superstructure remained unaltered. Over the next two years, the ship began to deteriorate dramatically under arid climatic conditions with temperatures soaring to 50°C at times. Externally, bleached paint began to flake off from the side of the dilapidated ship. Internally, as the consequence of neglect and lack of maintenance, on-board systems began to fail and were not repaired. Conditions became so bad that the ship was considered as a health hazard,with blocked toilets and drains, burst leaking pipes and internal plumbing. A shipping enthusiast visitor from the United Kingdom discovered that some parts of the ship smelt beyond belief and was totally infested with a plague of flies. Furthermore, in order to ventilate the ship, some of the glass panels and portholes had liberally been removed and several doors were damaged or missing. The ship was in a very depressing and dilapidated state.

Deserted and derelict, the sad sight of the TS *Bremen* in her final guise as the *Filipinas Saudi 1* at Jeddah in May 1980, looking forgotten and forlorn. (William Paulus)

Philsimport International Filipinas Saudi 1 1980

(Phillipine flag)

By the spring of 1980, the Saudi Arabian construction project had been completed. The ship was said to be almost uninhabitable and it was decided to dispose of it for scrapping to Philsimport International. The name of the ship changed to *Filipinas Saudi 1.* What happened next in the final chapter of the ship's story has, and will remain, a matter of great debate. There is a myth that the ship allowed itself to die rather than be scrapped. Others questioned whether someone wanted the ship to sink in deep water. Some suggest that the loss of the ship was a possible insurance fraud. Perhaps the true cause of the ship sinking was the underlying poor condition of the ship when it was overtaken by severe storm-force weather conditions.

In an insurance assessment report (dated 5 August 1980) given to Lloyds of London by Captain H.A. Van Opzeeland and Radio Officer J.M. Matituni of the Panamanian flag Dutch tug *Sumatra,* an account of what happened on the ship's final voyage is provided.

On 21 May Captain H.A. Van Opzeeland took command of the tug *Sumatra* with orders to tow the accommodation ship *Filipinas Saudi 1* from Jeddah to Taiwan for demolition. Later that day, Captain Van Opzeeland and Inspector Captain M. Mahon carried out a thorough inspection of the *Filipinas Saudi 1,* including all parts of the engine room, the pumps, helm, and four propeller shafts. All portholes were reported to be closed and all bulkhead watertight door and compartments were closed. Two pumps in the engine room were noted to be working normally. The ship was therefore certified safe to sail, with no likelihood of leaks.

The deserted *Filipinas Saudi 1* had her anchors raised at 5.08 a.m. GMT on the morning of 22 May and the three deck hands and pilot carefully climbed down the Jacob's ladder. The captain of the tug *Santania* then conducted a final independent visual inspection of the ship and confirmed that all was well via VHF radio. Only the pilot's Jacob's ladder remained hanging down from the ship.

Slowly, the Panamanian tug *Sumatra* hauled the ghostly *Filipinas Saudi 1* away from the quayside towards the invidious Taiwanese ship-breaking yard at Kaosiung, Taiwan. The voyage across the Red Sea went smoothly with no reported problems. On board the tug *Sumatra,* the fridge and on air conditioning system stopped. Radio Officer J.M. Matituni communicated the problem to the tugboat's owners who responded by advising the tug to call into Djibouti at the Horn of Africa for repairs. The tug and ship under tow arrived off Djibouti early on 27 May, where members of the tugboats crew climbed the pilot's Jacob's ladder, to drop anchor on the *Filipinas Saudi 1* at 7.25 a.m. Having anchored the ship, the tugboat headed off to Djibouti for repairs. Late the following day, 28 May, the tug rejoined the ship and reconnected the towing line ready to sail at 7.15 p.m. Slowly continuing across the Gulf of Aden, there were no reported problems, but it was observed that on occasions the ship very slightly listed first to starboard and then to port.

Weather reports transmitted to the tug *Sumatra* were routinely received, but no weather warning was conveyed. Frequent contact was kept with other shipping in the area to request weather report updates. The slow procession of the tug *Sumatra* and *Filipinas Saudi 1* passed north of the Island Socotra archipelago on the night of 2–3 June. On the morning of 3 June, the wind changed and began to blow from the south-west with a heavy swell.

The next day, on 4 June, an extra 200m of towing line was paid out to increase safety, because of the heavy swell, so that the ship now followed the tug at a distance of 1,100m. In view of the deteriorating weather conditions, a more southerly route was followed, but there were no problems encountered with the ship other than pitching in the waves.

As dawn broke on 6 June at 6.30 a.m. GMT, a storm began to develop of storm force 9 with a severe swell with 9–10m troughs between the waves. From the tug it was observed that the ship was listing at 5 degrees to port. It was impossible to launch a lifeboat from the tug to investigate why the ship was listing owing to the weather conditions. At midday, the position of the ship was 8 degrees 49 minutes north 57 degrees 31 minutes east and Radio Officer J.M. Matituni advised the Headquarters Office of the listing via VHF radio.

Throughout the hours of darkness during the night of 6–7 June, the tug trained a 3,000-watt beam of light on the ship to observe it. At 2.42 a.m. the position of the ship was 7 degrees 45 minutes north 57 degrees 12 minutes east and the south-westerly wind had slightly decreased to storm force 8 with a swell of 7–8m, but the listing on the ship had increased to 7 degrees to port. At 5.10 a.m. the twin engines on the tug were increased to 580rpm and a decision was made to head eastwards to better weather. As the sun rose in the sky, it was observed that the list of the ship had increased to 12 degrees, and the captain contacted his headquarters to inform them of the alarming developments. By midday, the barometer reading was 1004 and 1006mbps at storm force 9. Waves were now crashing over the forward deck of the ship and the list increased to 15 degrees.

During the night of 7–8 June the list of the ship increased alarmingly to 20 degrees. At daybreak, two lines of portholes on Decks D and C were submerged beneath the water line. The rear end of the ship was observed to be dipping, raising the bulbous bow at the stem of the ship above the water. A further communication from the tug to headquarters related that the sexton instrument had recorded that the ship was now listing at 22 degrees. By the afternoon this had increased further to 27 degrees.

Realising that the situation was now hopeless and dangerously out of control, with the permission of headquarters the tug Captain H.A. Van Opzeeland ordered the towing line to be cut at 1.15 p.m. Still the ship would not give up, and she lingered in the pains of death for one further night, but the following morning, on 9 June, with water now entering through the seacocks, she submitted to the inevitable and rolled over onto her port side at 4.46 a.m. GMT. Trembling and booming out in a cry of death, with a cloud of inky black soot defiantly pouring out of her funnel, the once great ship sank stern first beneath the waves in less than a minute at 4.47 a.m. GMT at position 7 degrees 53 minutes north and 60 degrees 21 minutes east. As the ship descended beneath the waves to a depth of 3,000m a dark maelstrom pool and debris boiled up at the surface and tangled waves swirled confusingly as gradually an eerie silence descended.

The tug *Sumatra* recovered three lifeboats, two life buoys and a few oddments of plywood. No human life had been lost when the ship went down, but sadly seven resident cats on the ship perished. Orders were received at 11.45 a.m. to cease searching on the tug and return to port.

At Lloyd's, London, the bell was rung. On 15 September 1980, the insurance payment was made for the total loss of the ship. In France, Britain and Germany, tears of grief ran down the cheeks of many who had served and travelled on this great ship of the seven seas, gone forever but never to be forgotten.

The original Compagnie de Navigation Sud Atlantique Paquebot *Pasteur* poster designed to launch the company's service to South America.

The launch platform plaque for the launch of the SS *Pasteur* at St Nazaire, which was retained as a souvenir and somehow survived the Second World War.

The commemorative medallion minted for the planned entry into service of the SS *Pasteur* in 1939. The front shows the ship while the back shows the French scientist Louise Pasteur after whom the ship was named.

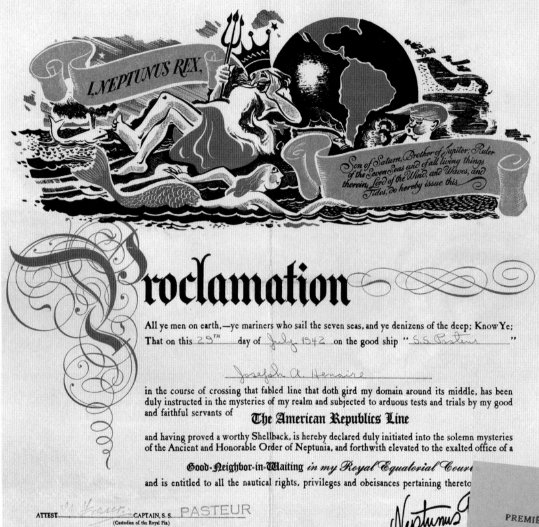

King Neptune certificate from the SS *Pasteur*, dated 29 July 1942, during the Second World War.

Paquebot "Pasteur"

MENU PREMIÈRE CLASSE

PETIT DÉJEUNER
Chocolat Café Lait - Pain
Thé - Confiture

DÉJEUNER
Hors-d'Œuvre
Omelette Grand'Mère
Petits Pois Paysanne
Tournedos Grillé Maître d'Hôtel
Salade de Saison
Fromage
-:- Glace au Chocolat -:-
Fruit

DINER
Consommé Froid
Chou-Fleur au Beurre
Jambon d'York aux Piccalilli
Salade Caprice
Fruit

Mercredi, 25 Décembre 1946.

The New Year Celebration programme of events for 1947 aboard the SS *Pasteur*.

The Christmas Day SS *Pasteur* first-class menu, dated Monday 25 December 1946.

PROGRAMME

PREMIÈRE PARTIE

1 - Tour de France folklorique
2 - Un peu de galéjades
3 - Yves Pallion et ses chansons
4 - Souplesse et Force
5 - En parlant un peu de Paris
6 - Mlle Brailly dans son tour de chant
7 - Intermède musical
8 - Bel Canto

ENTRACTE

DEUXIÈME PARTIE

1 - La Fontaine en Angleterre et à Paris
2 - Le marin chanteur
3 - Un peu de musique classique
4 - Mlle Lefèbvre dans son tour de chant
5 - Le jeu de la glace
6 - Virtuose Accordéoniste
7 - Billevesées
8 - Georgevail dans son répertoire

Avec tous nos meilleurs souhaits et vœux pour l'Année 1947

The front cover of the North German Lloyd 'This is the TS *Bremen* booklet', 1959.

Philatelic commemorative SS *Pasteur* First Day cover and stamp, dated 9 May 1954.

QUATRIÈME BOURSE PHILATÉLIQUE DE LA MÉDITERRANÉE
MARSEILLE 8-9 MAI 1954

THIS IS THE

'BREMEN'

FLAGSHIP OF THE NORTH GERMAN LLOYD

FACTS ABOUT THE BREMEN

Here are some interesting details about the "BREMEN" – fifth in the historic line to bear this proud name in the North German Lloyd Fleet.

VITAL STATISTICS. Her overall length is 699.6 feet, with a beam (maximum width) of more than 88 feet. There are 12 decks, including the Sun Deck, and from keel to top mast she is over 178 feet high – as tall as a seventeen story building. She registers 32,000 gross tons.

The "BREMEN" is a quadruple-screw turbine ship; her engines are capable of developing 60,000 horsepower, giving her a cruising speed of 23 knots. She crosses from New York to Cherbourg and Southampton in six days – to Bremerhaven in seven. She is air-conditioned throughout, and equipped with Denny Brown stabilizers to assure smooth sailing. The latest of nautical equipment and safety devices have been installed.

STAFF. 544 officers and men watch out for the comfort and safety of the "BREMEN'S" passengers. There are 4 chefs and 24 assistants – and 10 pastry cooks – in the ship's up-to-date kitchens. Altogether more than 300 service personnel cater to passengers' wishes in the kitchens, dining rooms, cabins, lounges etc.

The "BREMEN" anticipates all demands . . . fulfills all expectations. Above all, her staff is trained in the great tradition of Lloyd cuisine and Lloyd service – bywords for excellence in the world of travel.

PASSENGER ACCOMMODATIONS. All first class cabins have telephones, making possible ship-to-shore connections. There are accommodations for 1,200 passengers in all: more than 200 in First Class and over 900 in Tourist Class. 80 per cent of the staterooms are single or double; most of them have private facilities. All staterooms have one or more 110 V electric shaver outlets, and an electric-bell system for prompt, efficient service.

BEAUTY AND HEALTH FACILITIES. There are 2 beauty parlors and cosmetics salons, 2 barber shops, a swimming pool, Finnish and Medicinal Baths. There is a roomy gymnasium, massage rooms with sun lamps, and a fully-equipped hospital including X-rays.

SPECIAL FACILITIES. Executives traveling aboard the "BREMEN" can pursue their business activities with the help of typists and dictating machines. There is a travel office and a photo laboratory. The laundry and steam pressing valet service are at the guests' disposal. A "Special Travel Service" watches over passengers traveling alone or for the first time, elderly people and unaccompanied children. Kennels are available for pets.

FIRST CLASS PUBLIC ROOMS. Large Social Hall with dance floor, Dining Room, Library, Reading, Writing Room, Card Room, Cocktail Lounge and Bar, Taverne, Theatre, Nursery and Children's Playground.

TOURIST CLASS PUBLIC ROOMS. Large Social Hall with dance floor, Dining Room, Shopping Center, Veranda with dance floor, Lounge, two Writing Rooms, Cocktail Lounge and Bar, Library – Reading Room, Card Room, Taverne, Theatre, Nursery and Children's Playground.

FULL-VIEW PROMENADE DECK WINDOWS. Exceptionally large windows on Promenade Deck in both classes give excellent view of the sea while reclining in deck chairs.

DECKS. The one streamlined smokestack leaves maximum top-side space, and both classes have open-air sports and sun decks. The walk-around Tourist Class Promenade Deck covers 908 feet – 6 times equal one mile!

ELEVATORS. There are six passenger elevators to speed the guests between decks. Among the three other general service elevators is one especially designed for passenger cars to assure their loading and unloading in perfect safety.

North German Lloyd 'This is the TS *Bremen*' booklet, 1959.

The front cover of the North German Lloyd TS *Bremen* maiden voyage card.

Below left: The interior of the North German Lloyd TS *Bremen* maiden voyage card.

Below: North German Lloyd TS *Bremen* drinks place mat.

Here she is . . . a truly Fair Lady

The new "B R E M E N" fulfills all expectations, satisfies all demands,

large comfortable staterooms, spacious decks,
tastefully appointed luxurious public rooms, complete air-condition,
the latest technical improvements, modern stabilizers
and above all the traditional LLOYD cuisine and service,
bywords in transatlantic travel.

Maiden Voyage New York to Cherbourg, Southampton, and Bremerhaven July 21, 1959

and thereafter August 14, September 4, September 25, October 16,
November 6, November 26, and December 15.

NORTH GERMAN  LLOYD

Sailing the Seven Seas Since 1857

Printed in Germany

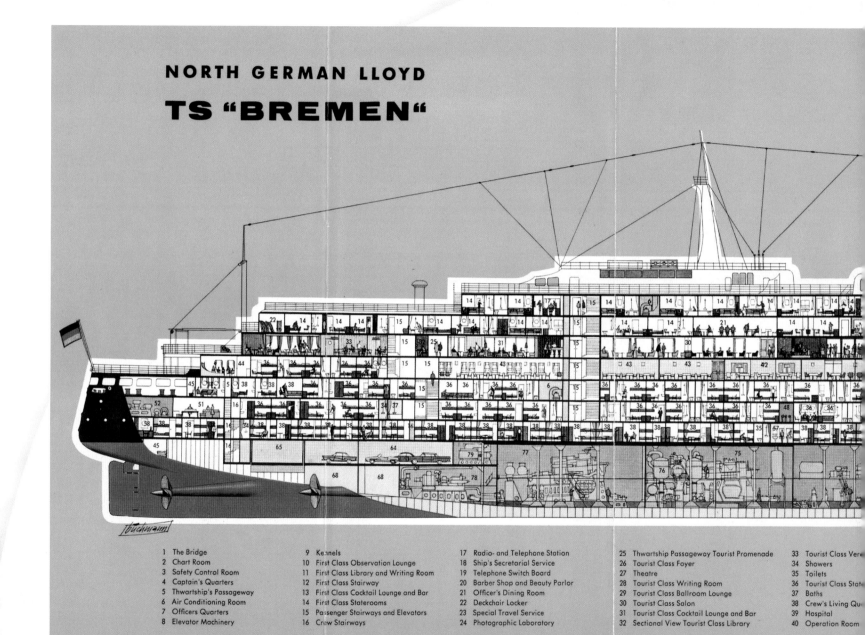

NORTH GERMAN LLOYD
TS "BREMEN"

1 The Bridge
2 Chart Room
3 Safety Control Room
4 Captain's Quarters
5 Thwartship's Passageway
6 Air Conditioning Room
7 Officers Quarters
8 Elevator Machinery
9 Kennels
10 First Class Observation Lounge
11 First Class Library and Writing Room
12 First Class Stairway
13 First Class Cocktail Lounge and Bar
14 First Class Staterooms
15 Passenger Stairways and Elevators
16 Crew Stairways
17 Radio- and Telephone Station
18 Ship's Secretarial Service
19 Telephone Switch Board
20 Barber Shop and Beauty Parlor
21 Officer's Dining Room
22 Deckchair Locker
23 Special Travel Service
24 Photographic Laboratory
25 Thwartship Passageway Tourist Promenade
26 Tourist Class Foyer
27 Theatre
28 Tourist Class Writing Room
29 Tourist Class Ballroom Lounge
30 Tourist Class Salon
31 Tourist Class Cocktail Lounge and Bar
32 Sectional View Tourist Class Library
33 Tourist Class Vera
34 Showers
35 Toilets
36 Tourist Class State
37 Baths
38 Crew's Living Qu
39 Hospital
40 Operation Room

North German Lloyd TS *Bremen*, cutaway sectional diagram.

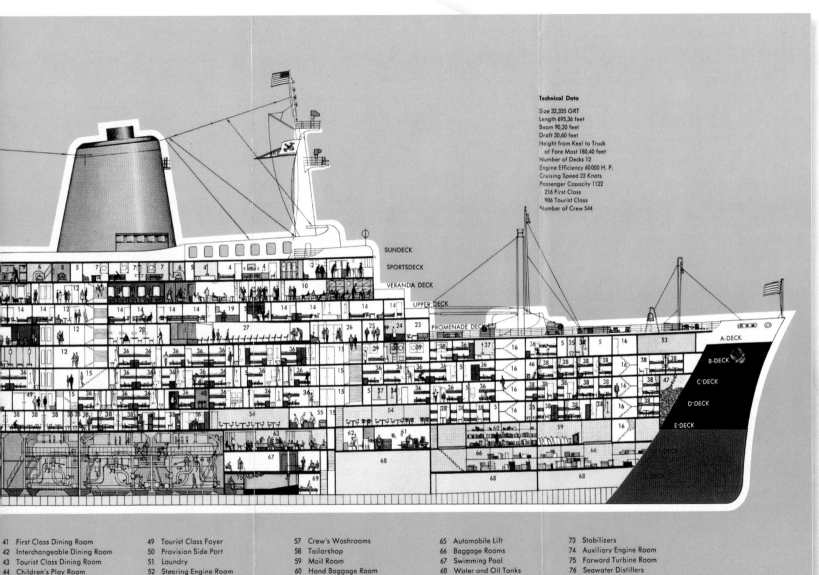

Technical Data

Size 32,335 GRT
Length 695,36 feet
Beam 90,20 feet
Draft 30,60 feet
Height from Keel to Truck
  of Fore Mast 180,40 feet
Number of Decks 12
Engine Efficiency 60 000 H. P.
Cruising Speed 23 Knots
Passenger Capacity 1122
  216 First Class
  906 Tourist Class
Number of Crew 544

SUNDECK
SPORTSDECK
VERANDA DECK
UPPER DECK
PROMENADE DECK
A-DECK
B-DECK
C-DECK
D-DECK
E-DECK
F-DECK
G-DECK

41 First Class Dining Room	49 Tourist Class Foyer	57 Crew's Washrooms
42 Interchangeable Dining Room	50 Provision Side Port	58 Tailorshop
43 Tourist Class Dining Room	51 Laundry	59 Mail Room
44 Children's Play Room	52 Steering Engine Room	60 Hand Baggage Room
45 Store Rooms	53 Anchor Windlass Engine Room	61 Printing Shop
46 Stock Room	54 Crew's Mess	62 Crew's Barber Shop
47 Chain Locker	55 Crew's Kitchen	63 Tavern
48 Fuel Oil Connections	56 Crew Purser's Office	64 Garage

65 Automobile Lift	73 Stabilizers
66 Baggage Rooms	74 Auxiliary Engine Room
67 Swimming Pool	75 Forward Turbine Room
68 Water and Oil Tanks	76 Seawater Distillers
69 Massage Rooms	77 After Turbine Room
70 Steam Baths	78 Turbo Generator
71 Main Boiler	79 Air Conditioning Compressors
72 Donkey Boiler	80 Double Bottom Tanks

A selection of TS *Bremen* menu card front covers.

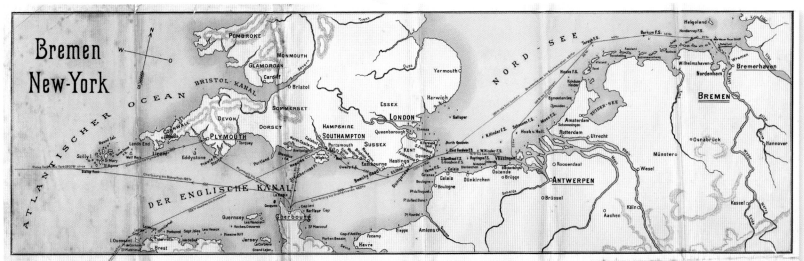

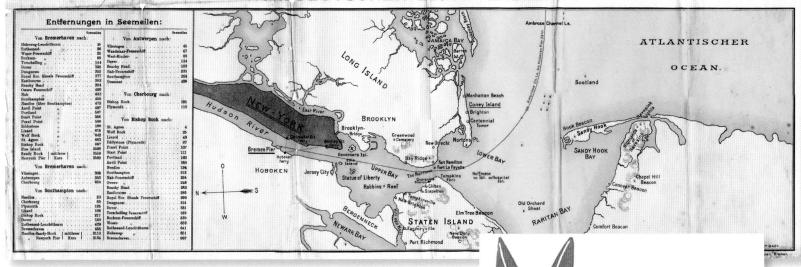

This unique item was a familiar sight to the scores of officers and crew of the TS *Bremen*, the original map of the bridge from the TS *Bremen* for the North Atlantic service, now preserved in the Britton Collection.

Easter Greetings from aboard the »Bremen«

Cover of an Easter card from the TS *Bremen*.

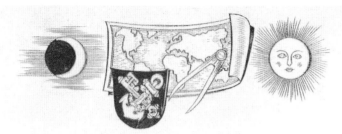

T.S. »BREMEN«

Frühstück	*Breakfast*
Früchte	**Fruits**
Grape Fruit - Äpfel - Orangen - Bananen	Grape Fruit - Apples - Oranges - Bananas
Gekühlte Pfirsiche mit Sahne	Ice Chilled Peaches with Cream
Gedünstete Früchte	**Stewed Fruits**
Pflaumen - Äpfel - Gemischtes Backobst	Prunes - Apples - Mixed Stewed Fruits
Fruchtsäfte	**Juices**
Orangen - Grape Fruit - Ananas - Tomaten	Orange - Grape Fruit - Pineapple - Tomato
Mehlspeisen	**Cereals**
Haferflocken in Milch - Haferschleim	Porridge in Milk - Oatmeal Gruel
Grape Nuts - Corn Flakes - Puffed Rice	Grape Nuts - Corn Flakes - Puffed Rice
Grieß in Milch - Shredded Wheat	Semolina in Milk - Shredded Wheat
Brot und Keks	**Bread and Rolls**
Brötchen - Weißbrot - Schwarzbrot	Fresh Rolls - White Bread - Black Bread
Graubrot - Knäckebrot - Zwieback	Rye Bread - Health Bread - Zwieback
Achimer Simon's Vollkornbrot	Achimer Simon's Vollkornbrot
Fisch	**Fish**
Gerösteter Kippered Hering	Broiled Kippered Herring
Geräucherter Schellfisch, Zerlassene Butter	Finnan Haddie, Drawn Butter
Eier	**Eggs**
Gekochte - Rühreier	Boiled - Scrambled
Spiegeleier mit Speck oder Schinken	Fried Eggs with Bacon or Ham
Poschierte Eier auf Toast	Poached Eggs on Toast
Deutscher Pfannkuchen	German Pancake
Vom Grill	**From Grill**
Amerikanischer Frühstücksspeck	American Breakfast Bacon
Koburger Schinken	Coburg Ham
Hausmacher-Bratwurst	Home-made Country Sausage
Fleischspeisen	**Meat**
Corned Beef Haschee mit Setzei	Corned Beef Hash with Fried Egg
Kalbsleber Sauté á la Minute mit Pilzen	Calf's Liver Sauté á la Minute w. Mushrooms
Kartoffeln	**Potatoes**
Gekochte - Püree- - Lyoner	Boiled - Mashed - Lyonnaise
Kalte Speisen	**Cold Dishes**
Frische und Geräucherte Deutsche Wurst	Fresh and Smoked German Sausages
Verschiedener Käse - Crackers	Boiled Ham - Cold Roast
Gekochter Schinken - Aufschnitt	Assorted Cheese - Crackers
Marmelade - Konfitüre - Gelee - Honig	Jam - Confiture - Jellies - Strained Honey
Getränke	**Beverages**
Kaffee - Tee - Kaffee Hag	Coffee - Tea - Kaffee Hag
Kakao - Schokolade - Frische Milch	Cocoa - Chocolate - Fresh Milk
Gesundheitstee	**Tisane**
Pfefferminz - Kamille - Lindenblüten	Peppermint - Camomile - Linden Blossom

TS *Bremen* breakfast menu card.

Lunch

Bielefeld Meat Salad - Sea-salmon in Oil - Marinated Fried Herring
Hearts of Artichokes Vinaigrette - Spanis Fish Salad - Eggs on Tomatoes
Fillet of Limandes Provençale - Ripe and Green Olives - Table Celery

Chicken Soup with Rice and Asparagus

Boiled North-sea Haddock, Sauce St.-Malo
Parsley Potatoes

Hungarian Paprika Gulyas with Tomatoes
Macaroni, Parmesan   Steamed Potatoes
Escarole Salad, Tarragon Dressing

French Cheese Cake

Fresh Fruit in Season

Coffee

To Order

Soups	Chervil Cream Soup with Croûtons
	Consommé Double in Cup
Fish	Fried Bluefish Vera Cruziana
Entrées	Stuffed Cabbage, Cumin Sauce
	Moussaka à la Moldave
Cold Dishes	Corned Brisket of Beef, Potato Salad
	Assorted Cold Roast, Cornichons
	Choice of Fresh and Smoked Sausage
Salads	Tomato Lettuce Cucumber Cresson
Dressings	Swedish Plaza St.-Regis Dill
Vegetables	Young Carrots Fresh String Beans
	Cauliflower Italian Summer Squash Bretonne
Potatoes	Boiled Mashed Candied Sweet Hashed
Dessert	Chocolate Ice Cream, Wafers, Stewed Pears
Cheese	Herb Petit Suisse Harzer Limburg
	Coffee - Tee - Cacao - Kaffee Hag
	Peppermint - Camomile
4.00 p.m.	Coffee - Tea - Cake

T.S. "BREMEN"   **Tuesday, June 16th, 1964**

TS *Bremen* lunch menu card, 16 June 1964.

Cold Buffet

Beluga Malossol Caviar on Ice Block

Iced Melon with Grand Marnier

Pâté de Foie Gras Strasbourgoise, Gelée de Madère

Heligoland Lobster Bremen Style

Gaspé Salmon with Crawfish-tails

Rainbow Brook-trout in Wine Aspic

Mediterranean Langouste Bellevue

Golf Shrimps Louisiana

Smoked Rhine Salmon Weser Eel and Wolga Sturgeon

American Prime Ribs of Beef, Sauce Tartare

Smoked Ox-tongue, Sauce Cumberland

Oregon Tom Turkey, Cranberry Sauce

Stuffed Eggs Rossini

Bresse Poularde, Salad Lorraine

Squab Pigeon and Rock Cornish Game Pullet Kalvill

Nantaise Duckling Bigarade

Saddle of Venison Baden-Baden

Westphalian Ham, Brunswick Asparagus Vinaigrette

Coburg Ham with Mayonnaise Salad

Black Forest Cherry Tart   Berlin Tart

Truffle Tart   Pralinés   Petits fours

Pyramid Cake

S.S. »BREMEN«   Monday, July 25th, 1960

Chef's Suggestion

Fresh Fruit Cocktail with Grand Marnier

Beluga Malossol Astrakhan Caviar

Blinis   Smetane

Green Turtle Soup Key West

Fresh Lobster à la Newburg

American Prime Ribs of Beef, Jus

Yorkshire Pudding   Creamed Horse-radish

Buttered Fresh String Beans   Pommes frites

Iceberg Salad, Thousand Island Dressing

Cauliflower with Parmesan and Butter

Ice Bomb "Bremen"

Assorted Cheese   Crackers   Radishes

Fresh Fruit in Season

Mocha

1st Bremen Cruise 1965

to the Caribbean

January 19 to February 2, 1965

NORTH GERMAN LLOYD

Sunday, January 31st, 1965

TS *Bremen* cold buffet menu card, 25 July 1960.

TS *Bremen's* first Caribbean Cruise Chef's suggestion menu card, Sunday 31 January 1965.

Farewell Dinner

à la Carte

Cocktails	Shrimp Cocktail Tomato Cocktail Fresh Fruit Cocktail with Grand Marnier
Hors-d'œuvre	Beluga Malossol Astrakhan Caviar Blinis Smetana Appetit Sild Bismarck Herring Baby Artichokes Vinaigrette Tuna in Oil Smoked Sturgeon Langouste in Mayonnaise Smoked Scotch Salmon Chicken Salad Marguerite Ripe and Green Olives
Soups	Green Turtle Soup Key West Chicken Cream Soup Princess Consommé Double Jubilée
Fish	Fresh Lobster à la Newburg Fried Rainbow-trout Meunière
Special Dish today	Sweetbreads Sauté, Sauce Béarnaise Petits-pois Française Parisian Potatoes

Entrées	American Prime Ribs of Beef, Jus
	   Yorkshire Pudding Creamed Horse-radish
	   Buttered Fresh String Beans Pommes frites
	   Iceberg Salad, Thousand Island Dressing
	Roast Oregon Tom Turkey, Giblet Sauce
	   Sage and Onion Stuffing Corn Fritters
	   Palm Beach Salad

Grill (10 Minutes)	London Mixed Grill Lamb Chops Carvalho
Cold Dishes	Pâté de Foie Gras Strasbourgoise, Gelée de Madère Saddle of Venison, Red Bar-le-Duc Long Island Duckling, Mashed Apples Philadelphia Capon, Knickerbocker Salad Smoked Westphalian Ham Glazed Coburg Ham
Salads	Asparagus Belgian Endive Pepper Cucumber
Dressings	Plaza Astor Orange Lorenzo Ginger
Vegetables	Cauliflower with Parmesan and Butter Creamed Fresh Spinach Broccoli Purée of Carrots Fried Egg-plant
Potatoes	Boiled Mashed Impérial Sweet Pont Neuf Straw
Dessert	English Raisin Cake Orange Custard Wine Crème Roulade
Compote	Sliced Hawaiian Pineapple Compote of Green Gages
Ice Cream	Ice Bomb "Bremen" Hazelnut Ice Cream Neapolitan Ice Cream Ice Punch Bonanza Wafers Friandises Chocolate Sauce
Cheese	Philadelphia Cream Chester Roquefort Bel Paese Gouda Fresh Fruit in Season
Coffee	Bremen "Special" - American - Instant Postum - Kaffee Hag - Nescafé
Tea	Darjeeling Flowery Orange Pekoe - Lipton - Ceylon Broken Orange Pekoe

11.30 p.m.:   **GALA BUFFET**

If desired special Dishes for Diet may be ordered!

TS *Bremen* Farewell Dinner
menu card.

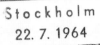

Stockholm
22. 7. 1964

NORDDEUTSCHER LLOYD BREMEN

BREMEN
KREUZFAHRT
1964
NORDSEE-OSTSEE
vom 17.- 25. Juli
KRÖNUNG
DER LLOYD SEEREISEN

Herrn
Karl Heinz Schmidt
7 Stuttgart Giebel
Mittenfeldstr. 119

TS *Bremen* First Day
postal covers, 1964 and
1966.

BREMEN

BREMEN
KREUZFAHRT

1966 ● ISLAND
● POLARKREIS
● NORWEGEN
vom 16. bis 24. Juli 1966
BREMERHAVEN - REYKJAVIK - AKUREYRI
HELLESYLT - MEROK - BERGEN
BREMERHAVEN

NORDDEUTSCHER LLOYD

Gerhard Ossenbrüggen
7082 OBERKOCHEN
Postfach 1
West - Germany

Left: TS *Bremen* First Day postal covers Christmas & New Year Cruise, 1969–70.

Right: TS *Bremen* ticket pocket, 15 November 1969.

Below: TS *Bremen* captain's invitation card, Wednesday 31 March 1971.

This Pocket contains
YOUR TICKET

for the T/S M/S ....BREMEN........................

Time of Embarkation: ..1..00..A.M. /P.M.

Date of Embarkation: ...Nov...15,.1969......

Sailing Time: ..4..00..P.M.....A.M./P.M.
New York local time

Sailing Date: ..Nov...15,...1969.......

NEW YORK · PIER 92
FOOT OF WEST 52ND STREET

This ticket and your passport (check expiration date) must be presented at the embarkation desk on the pier before boarding the vessel at the time of embarkation specified above.

IMPORTANT

Porters are available on the pier in New York to assist passengers with their baggage. This service is paid for by NORTH GERMAN LLOYD. Any demand for extra payment made by a porter should be reported immediately to the Baggage Master, Room 8, or to the Company's representative on the pier, with the badge number of the porter concerned.

NORTH GERMAN LLOYD
New York Office

Captain Paul Vetter
Commander, TS Bremen

Arthur Thomas
Cruise Director

request the pleasure of your company at the

Repeaters Party

Wednesday March 31st 1971 6.30 to 7.30 p.m.

in the Observation Lounge

Veranda Deck

Above: TS *Bremen* Cruise ticket, 15 November 1969.

Right: TS *Bremen* 'Your way to the USA' postcard.

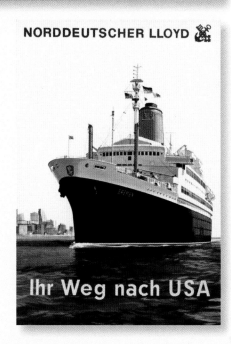

Above: TS *Bremen* cruise plan.

Left: TS *Bremen* souvenir log voyage 58, westbound, North Atlantic, June 1962.

Abstract of Log
S.S. »BREMEN«
32335 GRT · Length: 702 feet · Beam: 90 feet
Captain Günter Rössing

58th Voyage – Westbound – June 8th, 1962
from Bremerhaven to New York

June	Noon-Position Latitude North	Longitude West	Miles	Wind	Remarks
8	Bremerhaven		32	West 2	Departure 12.00 p.m., 02.30 p.m. passed Weser Light Vessel
9	Southampton		414	calm	Cloudless, smooth sea Arrival 10.36 a.m., Departure 01.42 p.m. Cloudless, calm sea
9	Cherbourg		81	calm	Arrival 06.00 p.m., Departure 09.00 p.m. Some clouds, calm sea
10	49° 51'	11° 03'	369	N to W 2-3	Cloudless, smooth sea
11	48° 19'	25° 32'	576	NW 3	Some clouds, smooth sea
12	45° 18'	38° 41'	570	SW 5	Mostly overcast, moderate sea
13	41° 51'	50° 53'	569	SW 1-2	Fog, calm sea
14	40° 52'	63° 04'	552	SW 3	Overcast, smooth sea
15	New York		516	West 2	Cloudless, smooth sea
	Total		3679		

June 15th, 1962, 10.30 a.m. passed Ambrose Light Vessel
Total Distance from Bremerhaven to New York: 3679 Nautical Miles

TS *Bremen* first-class menu.

North German Lloyd brochure cover.

North German LLoyd TS *Bremen* Carribbean cruise brochure.

TODAY'S TREASURE OF PLEASURE

Cruise to the Caribbean

March 24th – April 3rd 1971

Hapag-Lloyd AG
North German Lloyd Passenger Agency Inc. Gen. Agt.

TS *Bremen* cruise menu
cover.

GEPÄCKRAUM

TOURISTEN KLASSE

TOURIST-CLASS

Name
Schiff
Vessel
Kabine
Stateroom

NORDDEUTSCHER LLOYD BREMEN

Abfahrtsdatum
Sailing date

Abfahrtshafen
Port of departure

Bestimmungshafen
Port of destination

BAGGAGE ROOM

496-4689/5

KABINE

ERSTE KLASSE

FIRST-CLASS

Name
Schiff
Vessel
Kabine
Stateroom

NORDDEUTSCHER LLOYD BREMEN

Abfahrtsdatum
Sailing date

Abfahrtshafen
Port of departure

Bestimmungshafen
Port of destination

STATEROOM

TS *Bremen* luggage
labels.

TS *Bremen* cruise brochure cover.

ABSTRACT OF LOG

TS › BREMEN ‹

32 360 GRT · LENGTH 697 FEET · BEAM 90 FEET

CAPTAIN CARL OTTO EFFEROTH, Commander

June 22nd from Bremerhaven to New York

June 1971	Noon-Position Latitude North	Longitude West	Nautical Miles	Wind	Remarks
22	Bremerhaven			WNW 7	Departure 12.06 pm 2.36 pm passed Weser-Light-Vessel cloudy, very rough sea
23	Southampton		473	S 2	Arrv. 10.30 am Dep. 12.24 pm Variable cloudiness smooth sea
23	Cherbourg		95	calm	Arrv. 6.00 pm Dep. 8.30 pm Variable cloudiness smooth sea
24	49° 52'	11° 07'	368	SW 4	Overcast, slight sea
25	49° 12'	25° 16'	548	WNW 7	Overcast very rough sea
26	46° 39'	38° 25'	550	WNW 7	Variable cloudiness very rough sea
27	4° 10'	51° 06'	556	W 5	Variable cloudiness slight sea
28	41° 30'	63° 40'	575	NW 3	Sunny and clear skies slight sea
29	New York		496	W 3	Arrival 01.00 pm
		Total	**3661**		**Nautical Miles**

June 29th, 1971, 10.30 am passed Ambrose Lightvessel

Total Distance from Bremerhaven to New York : 3661 Nautical Miles

TS *Bremen* Atlantic log June 1971.

Auszug aus dem

Schiffstagebuch Souvenir Log

Turbinenschiff

› BREMEN ‹

NORDDEUTSCHER LLOYD
BREMEN

TS *Bremen* log.

This Sud Atlantique watercolour painting is an artist's impression of the SS *Pasteur*'s first-class lounge and smoking room. Of interest on the immense mahogany pillars is the hand-carved inlaid map which depicts the path of the intended regular voyages across the South Atlantic. It is said that this room was one of the most attractive afloat, rivalling even the Cunard Queen liners. Deep club chairs with blue and white fern-patterned upholstery floated on a sea of midnight blue wall-to-wall carpeting. The ambiance of sheer luxury in this room was completed by a series of zodiac symbols and nautical themes by the renowned French artist Le Bourgeots. (Britton Collection)

A Sud Atlantique watercolour artist's impression of the SS *Pasteur*'s second-class passenger lounge and bar. Of special interest are the black glass wall and chromium oxide metal bar covering. (Britton Collection)

This unique colour slide is believed to have been taken at 11 a.m. on 11 June 1940 and shows the SS *Pasteur* shortly after arrival from Brest at the West 48th Street Pier, New York, under the command of Captain François-Marie Petiot. She is seen here painted in light wartime grey livery and is fitted with light armaments. (Richard Weiss Collection)

A Sud Atlantique watercolour artist's impression of the SS *Pasteur*'s luxurious indoor swimming pool with the 27ft-high green ceramic sculpture entitled, 'Flora and Fauna of America'. The glass ceiling and brick-coloured glazed walls and floor conveyed a feeling of warmth and sheer luxury. There were two separate sunbathing areas for ladies and gentlemen, with panoramic sea views. (Britton Collection)

An impressive sea-level view taken from across the Hudson River at New York on 11 June 1940 with Manhattan in the background. From left to right: the Cunard liner RMS *Queen Elizabeth*, French Line SS *Normandie* and Sud Atlantique SS *Pasteur*. Although much smaller in size, the *Pasteur* stands out with her enormous funnel. (Richard Weiss Collection)

Far left: A view from the deserted Italian Line Pier looking along the Manhattan waterfront, taken on 11 June 1940, showing the funnels and masts of the Cunard liner RMS *Queen Elizabeth*, French Line SS *Normandie* and Sud Atlantique SS *Pasteur*. (Richard Weiss Collection)

Left: The HMT *Pasteur* is seen to be almost overflowing with Allied troops bound for the North African desert war campaign against Rommel's Afrika Korps. (William Tilley Collection)

Below: A deck scene aboard the HMT *Pasteur* shows brave, smiling Royal Canadian troops in their shorts, equipped with rifles, sailing from Halifax bound for El Alamein in North Africa. (Britton Collection)

Right: The HMT *Pasteur* is manoeuvred by a lone tugboat packed with Allied troops bound for the North African desert war campaign against Rommel's Afrika Korps. (William Tilley Collection)

Left: French troops disembark from the SS *Pasteur* at the quayside during the Indochina conflict. (Britton Collection)

Below: The inbound TS *Bremen* is seen passing a Moran tugboat on the Hudson River in November 1970. (David Boone/ Britton Collection)

Below left: This staged North German Lloyd publicity shot shows the SS *Berlin* passing the TS *Bremen* on the Hudson River off the battery in July 1959. This was the first time that two German liners were together in New York since the summer of 1939. The 19,100-ton *Berlin* was the former 1925-built *Gripsholm*, which was acquired by North German Lloyd in 1955. (North German Lloyd, New York Office Publicity Dept/Britton Collection)

Above left: A dramatic sea-level view taken from a tug shows the inbound TS *Bremen* under tow with her decks lined with excited passengers and crew on 5 August 1971. (Britton Collection)

Top right: The TS *Bremen* is gently nudged out into the Hudson River by a Moran tug after sailing from Pier 86 in New York on 22 December 1969. (Herb Frank/Richard Weiss Collection)

Above right: Dressed overall, the magnificent TS *Bremen* is gently turned down stream on the Hudson River in New York by a Moran tug. (Herb Frank/Richard Weiss Collection)

Left: The TS *Bremen* is underway, gently gliding downriver towards the open sea. (Britton Collection)

Left: The TS *Bremen* is cautiously moving up the Hudson River at 'dead slow ahead' as she approaches Pier 86 West 48th Street in New York in May 1971. (David Boone/Britton Collection)

Below left: An evocative portrait of the TS *Bremen* sailing up the Hudson River past the Day Line Pier in New York, seen passing the legendary Alexander Hamilton on 6 November 1971. (Braun Brothers/Britton Collection)

Below: Dressed overall, the TS *Bremen* is nudged out into the Hudson River from Pier 86 West 48th Street, New York, by a Moran tug in August 1969. The reflection of the ship shimmers in the ripples of the waves. (David Boone/Britton Collection)

Left: The TS *Bremen* gently eases her way out into the Hudson River followed by an attached Moran Towing tug. Meanwhile, moored at Pier 86 is the record-breaking holder of the Blue Ribanf, United States Line SS *United States*, which is having her fuel tanks replenished by Esso fules barges. (Herb Frank/Richard Weiss Collection)

Below: Captured to perfection between the piers at New York, Cunard RMS *Queen Elizabeth* escorted by a flotilla of Moran tugs makes her way slowly up the Hudson River to Pier 92, passing the SS *United States* at Pier 86 and the TS *Bremen* in 1968. (Bill Cotter)

Lights blaze out from the decks of the TS *Bremen* to illuminate the night sky along the Manhattan shoreline at Pier 86, West 48th Street. (Britton Collection)

New York Harbor port staff close off the portable ship-to-shore gangway between TS *Bremen* and Pier 88 prior to sailing. (Britton Collection)

The view from the port-side flying bridge on TS *Bremen*, looking back aft along the lifeboat deck, in December 1970. (Britton Collection)

In this mid-Atlantic view from the lifeboat deck on the TS *Bremen* we can see a distant freighter bound for New York. (Britton Collection)

An unusual, neck-breaking view, looking up from sea level to the lifeboat deck of the TS *Bremen*. (Britton Collection)

The TS *Bremen* is slowly turned in Southampton Water after arriving from Bremerhaven in 1965. (Britton Collection)

The distinctive red-coloured top of a Cunard liner peeps over the top of the neighbouring pier next to the TS *Bremen*, which rests at Pier 88 in New York in September 1969. (David Boone/Britton Collection)

Dressed overall at Pier 88, West 48th Street on 5 May 1971, the TS *Bremen* has her fuel tanks replenished with Bunker C oil by Esso fuel barges. Behind, moored in the adjacent pier, is the Cunard *Franconia*, and her distinctive round-topped red-stripped funnel can be seen just peeping into the picture. (Herb Frank/Richard Weiss Collection)

'Let go forward and aft,' shouts the captain of the TS *Bremen* as she sets sail from Pier 88 at New York, assisted by the *Kathleen E* Moran tug. (David Boone/Britton Collection)

A white plume of steam drifts from the funnel of the TS *Bremen* at Pier 88, West 48th Street, New York, as the Hudson River is iced up in this freezing cold view taken in February 1962. (Braun Brothers)

The Hudson River appears to be covered in ice in this wintry scene taken on 29 January 1961 at Pier 86 West 48th Street. The outside temperature is below zero, with not a soul to be seen on the decks of the TS *Bremen*. Note that the ice can be seen covering the starboard bow anchor. (James Braynaert/Richard Weiss Collection)

Ice surrounds the TS *Bremen* as she rests at Pier 86, West 48th Street, New York, on 29 January 1961. Rust has penetrated through the stern of the ship and ice can be seen hanging from the starboard bow anchor. The Arctic conditions have prevented passengers from wandering the decks to gaze at the skyscrapers of Manhattan. (James Braynaert/Richard Weiss Collection)

Nocturnal illuminations at Pier 88, West 48th Street, New York, as the lights from the TS *Bremen* glow in the night sky on 13 July 1971. (Herb Frank/Richard Weiss Collection)

A beam of light from a Moran tug illuminates the side of the hull of the TS *Bremen* at Pier 88, West 84th Street, New York. (Herb Frank/Richard Weiss Collection)

Above left: The view from the bridge of the TS *Bremen* as she rests at anchor at Pier 88, West 48th Street, New York, in September 1969. (Britton Collection)

Above: A view along the starboard lifeboat deck of the TS *Bremen* as she rests at anchor at Pier 88, West 48th Street, New York, in September 1969. Behind is the backdrop of Manhattan and gas-guzzling automobiles and buses racing along the shoreline road. (Britton Collection)

Left: It must have been a hot day at Pier 86, West 48th Street, New York, when this picture was taken in August 1971, as many of those on deck on the TS *Bremen* have their shirts removed and some are in shorts. The ship's name, *Bremen*, with the port of registry, Bremen, are proudly painted on the port-side stern. (Britton Collection)

Lunch time at Pier 88, West 48th Street in May 1959, as the painters appear to have abandoned their planks at the front bow of the TS *Bremen* and are pictured chatting and relaxing along the bow handrails. This was not a job for the faint-hearted, as one required a good head for heights and nerves of steel. (Britton Collection)

A quayside view looking up to the flying bridge of the TS *Bremen* showing the ship-to-shore gangways at Pier 88 West 48th Street in May 1959. (Britton Collection)

Right: 'Smile for the camera,' shouts an onlooker on Pier 86. Friends, family and spectators cheer and wave to passengers on board the TS *Bremen* as she slowly reverses away from Pier 86 and into the Hudson River. The faces of those watching tell a story: some are sad, others excited, while some appear to be curious, watching the spectacle in awe and wonder. (Britton Collection)

Below: An aerial view of Luxury Liner Row in October 1967, with, from left to right, the Day Line steamer *Alexander Hamilton*, Home Line *Oceanic*, an unidentified United States Line freighter, the North German Lloyd TS *Bremen*, the twin-funnelled Italian Line *Michelangelo* and the Cunard RMS *Franconia*. (Britton Collection)

Below right: A final opportunity to sunbathe at the stern of the TS *Bremen* before docking at New York in 1970. (Britton Collection)

This was the view from the bridge of the TS *Bremen* looking forward over the bow in 1970. Note the bronze ship's bell, which was proudly and regularly polished to perfection by the crew. (Britton Collection)

Treacherous times in the North Atlantic as the bow of the TS *Bremen* crashes down into a trough and the waves cascade over the foredeck with a covering of spray in this December 1970 view. (Britton Collection)

The TS *Bremen* increases her speed after emerging from a North Atlantic storm and this view looks back along the port-side lifeboat deck at the storm-force weather. (Britton Collection)

The bridge notice board on the
TS *Bremen*. (Britton Collection)

With the ship at anchor, the captain of the TS *Bremen* has
invited those interested to visit the bridge. The response
was beyond all his expectations. (Britton Collection)

Above: A closer view of the starboard-side lifeboat deck on the TS *Bremen* as she approaches New York in December 1970. (Britton Collection)

Above right: The immaculately polished bridge of the TS *Bremen* at Pier 88, West 48th Street, New York, in November 1970. Everything that could be polished is glistening and the floor has an almost perfect mirror finish. (Britton Collection)

Right: A close up view of the TS *Bremen* lifeboat 11 reveals that it could carry 146 people. (Britton Collection)

Above: Life ring on the TS *Bremen*. (Britton Collection)

Above right: The clock shows that it is 2.20 p.m. on the promenade deck of the TS *Bremen* as passengers are pictured relaxing in their deck chairs and strolling along the vast deck. (Britton Collection)

Right: Coffee is served on the promenade deck of the TS *Bremen* as passengers relax and look out to observe the passing waves of the North Atlantic. (Britton Collection)

Top left: The oompah band of the TS *Bremen* strikes up a traditional rousing foot stomping Bavarian song for the passengers – so typical of this wonderful ship. (Britton Collection)

Top centre: A gentle wisp of steam drifts from the impressive straw-coloured funnel of the TS *Bremen* on 27 January 1961. When the polished whistles were sounded they could be heard for many miles. Their distinctive sound was heard by the author in his bed in Winchester, some 15 miles from Southampton Docks. (James Braynaert/Richard Weiss Collection)

Top right: A view from the aft sun deck looking forward to the funnel of the TS *Bremen*, which is clearly underway as clouds of black smoke are seen billowing from the enormous funnel. (Britton Collection)

Left: Passengers relax in their deck chairs. TS *Bremen* is underway, with black smoke pouring out of the funnel. (Britton Collection)

Left: The port-side shell door of the TS *Bremen* has been opened in readiness for the transfer of the Trinity House Pilot off the Nab Tower, near Bembridge, Isle of Wight, in 1966. (Britton Collection)

Below: This remarkable picture was taken from the Trinity House Pilot boat off The Nab Tower, near Bembridge, Isle of Wight, in 1966 as the TS *Bremen* lay at temporary anchor. The passengers look out from the promenade deck windows and the captain and officers peer down from the flying bridge of the TS *Bremen*. Above, screaming seagulls swirl around, hoping for tit-bits of food. (Britton Collection)

Below: The TS *Bremen* is gently manoeuvred by Red Funnel tugs in Southampton Water on 5 September 1971. (Marc Piche/ Britton Collection)

Right: The Alexander Towing Co. tug *Ventnor* heaves the TS *Bremen* into position at Southampton Docks on 22 September 1968. (George Garwood/World Ship Society)

The cooks and stewards line the stern deck as the Alexander Towing Co. tug *Ventnor* and Red Funnel tug *Calshot* heave the TS *Bremen* into position at Southampton Docks on 22 September 1968. (George Garwood/World Ship Society)

The TS *Bremen* has just arrived in Southampton Water from Bremerhaven and is pictured being readied for turning and docking on 22 September 1968. (George Garwood/World Ship Society)

Flocks of seagulls follow the TS *Bremen* as she docks at Southampton on 22 September 1968. They are no doubt attracted by tit-bits of food being thrown from the stern of the ship by the cooks and stewards who can be seen dressed in their white uniforms. (George Garwood/ World Ship Society)

The TS *Bremen* is pictured being turned in Southampton Water ready for docking on 22 September 1968. She is ably assisted by the Red Funnel tugs *Dunnose* and *Calshot* with extra support from the Alexander Towing tug *Ventnor*. To the left of the liner a chimney of Marchwood Power Station. (George Garwood/World Ship Society)

The TS *Bremen* slowly makes her way down Southampton Water in 1971, passing the *Fairstar*. (Gerald Trought/World Ship Society)

With towing lines firmly attached, the TS *Bremen* is inched out of Ocean Dock, Southampton, in 1971. (Gerald Trought/ World Ship Society)

Pictured from sea level on board a local pleasure craft, the TS *Bremen* is docked at 107 Berth in the New Docks at Southampton. Following this tourist tour of the Docks, the author and his family ventured aboard the TS *Bremen* and explored this superb liner from bridge to engine room. (John A. Britton/Britton Collection)

Docking of the TS *Bremen* at Bremerhaven in 1963. (Britton Collection)

The flagship of North German Lloyd, TS *Bremen*, is pictured at her home port at the Columbus Quay, Bremerhaven, in 1965. The dock cranes are busy at work loading the forward cargo hold. (Britton Collection)

Postcard of the TS *Bremen* smoking and games lounge. (Britton Collection)

TS *Bremen* at the Columbus Quay, Bremerhaven, in 1960. (Britton Collection)

The TS *Bremen* dining room. (Britton Collection)

The TS *Bremen* dance floor. (Britton Collection)

Postcard from the TS *Bremen*.
(Britton Collection)

The captain's table on
TS *Bremen*. (North
German Lloyd/Britton
Collection)

The TS *Bremen* chef's piece de resistance. (North German Lloyd/Britton Collection)

The TS *Bremen*'s finest lobster. (North German Lloyd/Britton Collection)

The TS *Bremen*'s tourist lounge bar. (North German Lloyd/Britton Collection)

The TS *Bremen*'s tourist lounge. (North German Lloyd/Britton Collection)

The Caribbean coast from the forward observation deck of TS *Bremen* in November 1970. (Britton Collection)

Arrival in paradise aboard the TS *Bremen*. A Caribbean cruise, November 1970. (Britton Collection)

The TS *Bremen* tender boat carries excited passengers ashore to an island in the West Indies. (Britton Collection)

TS *Bremen* Caribbean cruise publicity leaflet cover. (North German Lloyd/Britton Collection)

TS *Bremen* Caribbean cruise publicity photos. (North German Lloyd/Britton Collection)

Below left: TS *Bremen* at anchor off Trinidad. (North German Lloyd/Britton Collection)

Below right: At anchor off the Caribbean. (Richard Weiss Collection)

Viewed from the tender, passengers return to the ship from their Caribbean visit ashore, November 1970. (Britton Collection)

The TS *Bremen* at anchor in paradise off the Caribbean in November 1970. (Britton Collection)

A loving admirer of the TS *Bremen* looks on from on high in the Caribbean in November 1970. (Britton Collection)

A postcard view of the TS *Bremen* and Cunard RMS *Queen Elizabeth* at anchor at Curaçao during a Caribbean cruise. (Richard Weiss Collection)

Postcard view of the TS Bremen at anchor during a Caribbean cruise. (Britton Collection)

The TS *Bremen* is pictured entering Quebec in Canada in August 1971. (Marc Piche)

Right: A delightful aerial view of the TS *Bremen*, which was taken for the North German Lloyd Publicity Department. (North German Lloyd/Britton Collection)

Far right: The Chandris Line TS *Regina Magna* is pictured entering Southampton. (Barry J. Eagles)

The TS *Bremen* is pictured at Lee Ryan in Canada during a rare visit in August 1971. (Marc Piche)

LE JERSEY ✿ SAINTJOSEPH
en croisière à bord du Regina Magna

La Compagnie Chandris Cruises offre, en tant que compagnie spécialisée sur l'organisation de croisières, des possibilités multiples, un éventail de prix très étudiés et une gamme d'itinéraires. Vous pourrez découvrir la Méditerranée ou la Baltique, le Cap Nord, la mer Egée ou l'Atlantique et d'autres pays aussi extraordinaires.

Elles sont souples, légères, féminines, les petites robes en jersey Saint Joseph.
Ci-dessus : taille marquée, plis piqués tout le long du corps s'évasant à partir des hanches (env. 495 F).

LE JERSEY ✿ SAINTJOSEPH
en croisière
à bord du Regina Magna

Les nombreux bateaux de la Chandris offrent tous le même confort raffiné et les divertissements à bord. Aux escales, vous participerez si vous le désirez à des excursions prévues qui vous permettront d'apprécier l'aspect touristique, historique et culturel du pays.

Très à la mode cet été, le blanc. Saint Joseph vous propose deux modèles en jersey.
Pour la femme : pantalon évasé, chemise saharienne fendue sur le côté (env. 595 F). Pour l'homme : veste près du corps, poches plaquées (env. 835 F). A droite, à l'occasion d'une escale dans l'île pittoresque de Lanzarote aux Canaries, robe virevoltante, décolletée en jersey imprimé chatoyant (env. 600 F).

Magazine advertisement taken on board the Chandris Line TS *Regina Magna*. (Le Jersey Saint Joseph/Britton Collection)

Magazine advertisement taken on board the Chandris Line TS *Regina Magna*. (Le Jersey Saint Joseph/Britton Collection)

This dramatic sequence of the *Filipinas Saudi 1* sinking was taken from the tug *Sumatra* by Frans Schepers. On 9 June 1980, with water now entering through the sea cocks, she submitted to the inevitable and rolled over on to her port side at 4.46 a.m. GMT. Trembling and booming out in a cry of death, with a cloud of inky black soot defiantly pouring out of her funnel, the once great ship sank stern first beneath the waves in less than a minute at 4.47 a.m. GMT at position 7 degrees 53 minutes north and 60 degrees 21 minutes east. As the ship descended beneath the waves to a depth of 3,000m, a dark maelstrom pool and debris boiled up at the surface and tangled waves swirled confusingly, then gradually an eerie silence descended. (Frans Schepers)